THE
ROAR
OF THE LIONESSES

THE
ROAR
OF THE LIONESSES

Women's Football in England

Carrie Dunn

First published by Pitch Publishing, 2016

Pitch Publishing
A2 Yeoman Gate
Yeoman Way
Worthing
Sussex
BN13 3QZ

www.pitchpublishing.co.uk
info@pitchpublishing.co.uk

ISBN 978-1-78531-151-2

Typesetting and origination by Pitch Publishing

Printed by Bell & Bain, Glasgow, Scotland

Contents

Foreword

by Gillian Coultard

*Former England captain and winner of
119 international caps*

Twice National League champion, six-time Women's
FA Cup winner with Doncaster Belles
English Football Hall of Fame inductee, 2006

WHEN I began my career, women's football was still amateur. I enjoyed travelling the world a little bit, playing four England internationals a year, if that, and captaining the side, but the players now go further and further afield with their full schedules. Although it was great to see England's success at the Women's World Cup in Canada, there's still plenty of work to be done – both at the top level and at grassroots. The commitment of women throughout the football pyramid is and always has been impressive – from Moya Dodd, on the FIFA executive committee, to the players running their own clubs and scrabbling the money together for pitch hire. Their stories deserve to be heard.

Acknowledgements

This book has been a sheer joy to work on.

I owe thanks to very many clubs and people around the UK: Leyton Orient Women (especially Chris Brayford, Olympia Diamond and Danni Griffiths), Doncaster Belles (especially Faye Lygo and Courtney Sweetman-Kirk), Sheffield (especially Richard Tims, Helen Mitchell, Carla Ward, Lisa Giampalma and Jodie Michalska), Manchester City (especially Gavin Makel and the magnificent Sylvia Gore), Millwall Lionesses (especially general manager Hannah Burnett-Kirk and former general manager Charley Mitten), London Bees, Birmingham City Ladies, Cardiff City Ladies (especially Abbie Britton), Tottenham Hotspur Ladies, West Ham Ladies, AFC Unity (especially Jay Baker and Jane Watkinson), Goaldiggers (especially Fleur Cousens) and last but not least Arsenal Ladies (especially Rebecca James – one of my former students!).

Thanks also to Crissy Torkildsen of Coventry City Ladies, Matt Cecil at Wycombe Wanderers, Jon Horton, formerly of Reading Women, Carol West and Karen Falconer of the FA Women's Premier League, and Kelly Simmons of the FA.

Thanks to Gary Phillpott of Off The Fence theatre company.

Thanks to all the fans, players and administrators of women's football who shared their views with me, sometimes on condition of anonymity.

Thanks particularly to the legendary Gillian Coultard for agreeing to write the foreword; when I approached her to ask whether she might be prepared to do so, I explained that I thought it was vital for any book about women's football in England today to honour the work done by previous generations of players to get us where we are now. I am thrilled that someone who has made such a huge contribution to women's football has also contributed to this book.

The year in which I wrote this book was also the year my small nephew George went to his first football match (I talk about this in a later chapter). When I was reporting from the Women's World Cup in Canada, I Skyped him from one of the grounds in the second week of the tournament. Having already made me feel like a thoroughly neglectful aunt by scolding me sadly for being 'away for a long time', he then realised I was at a different stadium than the one I'd called from before, and asked me bewilderedly, 'Why are you at ANOTHER football ground? You've already BEEN to one!' I hope from this year onwards he starts to understand why I go to so many football matches around the world! This book is for him.

Prologue

IT'S a pleasantly warm August afternoon, and I'm at Wembley with tens of thousands of other football fans.

None of us are there to cheer on England's men, or any of the Premier League stars. It's the FA Women's Cup Final, held at the new national stadium for the very first time, and attended by 30,710 people.

I'm in the press box, as I often am for domestic women's football matches, but this time, rather than sharing the space with one or two others, the place is packed. I'm co-commentating for the radio, but we're not the only broadcast team there – there's a huge demand all over the country for live coverage and regular updates from this match. Former England internationals are serving as pundits on other stations; journalists unused to the women's game are ensuring their notes are all in order; it's a frantic and busy day.

I'm working, but there are dozens of my friends and relatives in the crowd enjoying a day out in north-west London. None of us has any allegiance to either Chelsea or Notts County, the two teams playing today, but everyone wanted to show their support for women's football after enjoying the Women's World Cup so much during the summer of 2015.

They weren't the only ones. Attendances at FA Women's Super League games – the elite domestic competition for women's football in England – increased by 48 per cent following the Women's World Cup, according to the FA's official figures.

I was lucky enough to fly out to Canada and follow England's progress, reporting on matches and interviewing players for a national newspaper as well as an international sports website. There weren't that many English journalists out there from the off, beginning with the group games in tiny east-coast town Moncton; after all, women's international football tournaments on another continent come fairly low down the news agenda priorities for sports desks.

It was the second Women's World Cup I had travelled to and written about, following 2011's tournament in Germany. The entire event in Canada felt a bit smaller than the exuberant, high-profile celebration of women's sport we'd had four years previously. Oddly, it also felt much more commercial; the sponsors' logos seemed much more prominent around the host towns and cities and within the stadia. Despite that, I was delighted that friends, colleagues and acquaintances – some of whom had never expressed interest in any sport before, let alone women's football specifically – were asking me about the tournament. The media coverage in England gathered momentum along with the team; Lucy Bronze's magnificent strike against Norway was replayed again and again on news bulletins and grabbed people's attention, and once they found themselves watching a match, they also found themselves caught up in a tournament they never expected to follow.

Not even the post-midnight kick-off times put them off. After England were knocked out of the tournament by Japan courtesy of a late Laura Bassett own goal, my phone began buzzing with texts and my social media notifications lit up, all from people in England who were watching the match and wanted to reflect on it. That was happening all around the UK; indeed, during the third-place play-off, the website for the FA Women's Super League crashed due to demand. Full-page adverts expressing support for the team were published in the latter stages of the tournament; the top of the BT Tower in London carried a good luck message on the day of the semi-final.

Towards the end of the tournament's group stages I had been a guest on a BBC Radio 5 Live programme with a panel of journalists who specialised in women's football; we all agreed that the team's target would be the quarter-finals and anything beyond that would be a bonus. England exceeded those expectations, finishing third and in the process beating Germany for the first time ever. It was no wonder that people wanted to go to Wembley and welcome back those players who'd been a key part of Mark Sampson's squad of Lionesses.

The FA Women's Cup Final was a delightful showpiece occasion, all in all. After it was over, with Emma Hayes's excellent Chelsea side lifting the trophy, I trekked up the road to catch my bus home, and hoped once more that the increased interest in women's football in England would continue.

*% *% *% *% *%*

In the mainstream media and the popular histories, women's football did not take off in England until 1993, when the FA took control of it. This narrative overlooks so much. It ignores the fact, first of all, that the governing body actually banned women from playing the game. After a warning issued to men's clubs in 1902, warning them not to play against 'ladies' teams', the edict was passed down in 1921 and the prohibition lasted for half a century.

The reasons for the ban were multiple. The FA's minutes record their rather stiffly expressed justifications thus:

> 'Complaints having been made as to football being played by women, the Council feel impelled

to express their strong opinion that the game of football is quite unsuitable for females and ought not to be encouraged.

'Complaints have also been made as to the conditions under which some of these matches have been arranged and played, and the appropriation of receipts to other than charitable objects.

'The Council are further of the opinion that an excessive proportion of the receipts are absorbed in expenses and an inadequate percentage devoted to charitable objects.

'For these reasons the Council request clubs belonging to the association to refuse the use of their grounds for such matches.'

'Unsuitable for females'? Perhaps this is the most predictable objection to women's sport; indeed, the allegation that sport is physically dangerous for women continues even in the 21st century. Gian-Franco Kasper, president of the International Ski Federation, was asked in 2005 about the limitations placed on women's ski jumping competitions, and he answered, 'It's like jumping down from, let's say, about two metres on the ground about 1,000 times a year, which seems not to be appropriate for ladies from a medical point of view.'

The financial objections remain intriguing and have still not been fully explained. It is almost certain that the FA were referring obliquely to the most famous women's team of the time, Dick, Kerr Ladies. A group of female workers at the factory enjoyed their kickarounds during their breaks, and in his office above, draughtsman Alfred Frankland saw an opportunity. He suggested that they form an organised team – and put himself forward as their manager.

The Dick, Kerr Ladies were more successful than anyone could have imagined. During the First World War, when the men's leagues were suspended, they (and teams like them) were attracting tens of thousands of fans to their matches – ostensibly to raise money for charities. Questions were, however, asked about the accounting practices of these clubs, as the FA's meeting appears to have done. Instead of asking to inspect the books, though, the FA issued a blanket ban on women playing football.

The Dick, Kerr Ladies were not even the first women's team. The intriguingly-pseudonymised Nettie Honeyball was the figurehead for the British Ladies, who played in the first recorded organised game of women's football back in 1895 (there were certainly games before that as well); this was held in London and contested between a team from the north and one from the south of England.

One plausible factor for the prohibition is not noted in the minutes, and that is the sheer success of women's football. Even after the Great War, the matches were still astonishingly popular. The Dick, Kerr Ladies took on St Helens Ladies at Goodison Park, the home ground of Everton, on Boxing Day 1920, in front of more than 53,000 people – with another several thousand hopeful attendees locked outside. Could it be that those governing English football were concerned that fans would be drawn to the women's game at the expense of the men's?

Whatever the genuine motives, the ban took effect; yet it did not destroy women's football. Women continued to play, regardless of the FA's decision to ignore their very existence. They could not play on proper football pitches so they found themselves playing at rugby clubs, or parks, or whatever piece of scrubland they could find. Men who helped the women's teams found themselves fined and suspended by the FA. Entirely separate from the governing body's control, women's football organised itself in the face of all these obstacles, forming the English Ladies' Football Association less than a week after the FA's declaration.

Dick, Kerr Ladies became essentially a representative England team as they toured the world, sporting a Union Flag image on their kit. They had assumed this role even before the FA's ban, taking on a team from Scotland in 1920 – and crushing them 22-0. In the years following the prohibition, Frankland's team continued to travel and play, often against men, simply because there were reasonably few female opponents for them.

That was because other countries were facing similar problems to England, with the men's federations across the world trying to ignore women's football as best they could, and having reasonable success in starving it into oblivion; indeed, by 1947, just after the end of the Second World War, reports suggest that there were fewer than 20 women's clubs left in England, making it nigh-on impossible to stage regular games, but also meaning it was difficult for women who were interested in playing to find a club. These local teams had to play mostly exhibition games against each other depending on availability of players and a venue – but they also got the opportunity to travel the globe and play against teams from other countries. Manchester Corinthians, for example, enjoyed lengthy trips to Germany, Portugal, Madeira, Italy and Tunisia.

England's men winning the World Cup in 1966 generated more interest in the game, including from women. As more wanted to play, more clubs were established, often attached to a workplace and making use of their recreational grounds, and local leagues slowly began to take shape. In the absence of UEFA bothering itself about women's matches, the Federation of Independent European Female Football was established to organise international tournaments. This was a quango of businessmen seeing a decent commercial opportunity and they promptly launched plans for cross-Europe competitions as well as global ones. Harry Batt, the manager of women's team Chiltern Valley, was the man they invited to put together an England side. This all came as the Women's FA – separate from the FA itself, which was finally reconsidering its ban, and thinking about allowing women's teams to affiliate and compete officially, just as men's teams did – began to put down roots. Initially calling itself 'the Ladies' Football Association of Great Britain', it very much wanted to establish an official England representative side rather than Batt's invitationals. At this time, though, some other European countries were proving themselves more forward-thinking – there were some places where it was even possible for women to play football for money, albeit a very small amount. The Women's FA, though, just as authoritarian as its male counterpart, ruled that players who wished to be selected for England must retain their amateur status and refuse any potential moves abroad.

The Women's FA might have been good at making rules but it was not so good at organisation – whether that was matches, travel, funds or resources. Its job was made even tougher, strangely, by the FA finally agreeing to lift the ban on the women's game in 1970, allowing matches at football grounds and permitting referees to officiate, because it took so long to actually put those recommendations into practice.

FIFA and UEFA also realised they had to agree to endorse women's football if they were not to lose control of the game entirely, what with the international tournaments organised by FIEFF, but they were still unsure about what format their support should take. The WFA was extremely nervous about the independent proposals for a Women's World Cup to be held in England in 1972 or 1973; FIFA and UEFA had already rejected the ideas, expressing a concern that such a showcase of women's football would simply 'earn money' rather than promote and advance the sport as a whole. That was not to say, of course, that UEFA or FIFA were proposing to organise anything formal themselves; rather, a series of invitational tournaments were set up, right up until 1991, when the first official Women's World Cup was held.

The last England international under the Women's FA's remit was in November 1992 against Italy as the FA finally started to take full control of women's football. It had taken the FA until 1983 to invite the Women's FA to affiliate to it and remain 'the sole governing body for women's football', but in the decade since then it had become increasingly clear that better processes were needed to give England a chance of success on the global stage – they had failed to qualify for the inaugural Women's World Cup, after all. More than that, though, the WFA was staffed by volunteers, who had their day jobs to fit in as well, and despite commitment to the cause and swathes of good intentions, that did not necessarily mean they were good at their roles in football administration.

The FA appointed Ted Copeland, the assistant regional director of coaching for the north-east, as the new manager of the England women's team, but the players themselves remained amateur, often ending up financially worse off after a match or a training camp with only a maximum of £15 a day in expenses on offer. Hope Powell was appointed in 1998, and radically restructured and revitalised women's football across all age groups with her overarching remit.

England hosted the 2005 European Championships, an opportunity to demonstrate the development of women's football under the FA's control. Yet the tournament received relatively little media coverage and the chance to bring the game to the mainstream and popularise it as a spectator sport, as well as create a legacy for participation, was lost.

A new strategy for women's football was needed. The decades of amateurism across the game were at an end. In 2011 the FA Women's Super League (WSL) was launched, with eight elite teams competing, and with four players in each of those squads receiving a maximum annual salary of £20,000, increased to £26,000 the year after. There were also central contracts on offer for England players, meaning the success of the domestic league was directly linked to the success of the national team from the start.

There were some features of the WSL that were confusing to onlookers. First, there was the application system – to take part, clubs had to formally apply for a licence, and initially there was no promotion or relegation, just a closed competition. After the first four years, a second division was created, and all the clubs applied once more – with Doncaster Belles, a solid mid-table team, bumped down to the new WSL2, and Manchester City, brand new but with vast money behind them, parachuted into WSL1. Second, there was the scheduling; it was intended to run over the summer months, to avoid clashes with the men's professional leagues, and built in a sizeable gap so as to allow for global competitions such as the Olympics, the European Championships and the Women's World Cup.

More than that, though, it ran at a different time of the year to the rest of the women's football pyramid. The Women's Premier League (WPL), organised in regional divisions and long the top division of elite women's football, had been superseded by the WSL, and maintained its normal August to May season; after all, with no promotion or relegation between the best and the rest, there was no need to alter it.

However, in 2015 the first WPL club was promoted to WSL2 after Northern WPL champions Sheffield Ladies and Southern WPL champions Portsmouth Ladies fought it out in a one-off play-off for the big time. With the possibility of the WSL and WPL properly linking up in the future, with promotion and relegation as a matter of course, the problem of the fixture scheduling remained high on the agenda for fans, players and administrators.

※ ※ ※ ※ ※

This is not a fully comprehensive chronicle of everything that has happened in women's football in the months since the Women's World Cup and the subsequent FA Cup Final. Rather, it is a glimpse into the lives of women's football clubs, players and administrators around the country, at all levels – a series of snapshots coming together to create a broader picture of the achievements of the game as well as the obstacles it still faces.

Autumn 2015

ENGLAND had played their last match in Canada on Saturday 4 July, flying back into London Heathrow on the Monday morning.

Five days later, domestic fixtures resumed in the Women's Super League, which had taken a break while the World Cup was on. Not all of the England players immediately returned to play but they did make appearances prior to their teams' matches, collecting bouquets, waving to the crowd, signing autographs and posing for photos. The accessibility and the down-to-earth presentation of the very best female footballers in the world have long been the most marketable qualities of the women's game; you're never going to get anywhere near the likes of Lionel Messi or Cristiano Ronaldo, or Harry Kane or John Terry, but Marta and Abby Wambach, Fran Kirby and Steph Houghton will always be happy to stop and have a chat with fans.

Some players came back from Canada with a slight knock, others were understandably tired after the rigours of tournament football and the emotional rollercoaster of the last-minute semi-final loss against Japan followed by the stunning win against Germany to secure a bronze medal. It was understandable that some observers wondered quite why the WSL began again so soon after the scheduled end of the tournament – weren't the powers-that-be expecting

England to get through to the final weekend in Canada? – but it had been set out on the calendar for months, and meant that clubs could quickly capitalise on the lure of the Lionesses to advertise their forthcoming matches. That only applied to WSL1, though; the second tier of WSL competition lost their only Lioness when Reading's Fran Kirby signed for Chelsea, generating a record transfer fee for English women's football at the same time.

So WSL1 benefited hugely from a post-World Cup attendance bounce. Manchester City secured a new home ground record when they attracted 2,102 fans to the Academy Stadium for their first game back after the summer break, beating Birmingham City 1-0 thanks to a goal from England's Toni Duggan (Arsenal had attracted over 5,000 fans to the Emirates Stadium in 2012 for a WSL match against Chelsea but that was a one-off special event).

'It wasn't full,' said Lucy Bronze, Duggan's club and international team-mate, immediately after the game, 'but it was fuller than we've had it. Maybe in a few seasons we'll start selling the place out.'

Bronze was certainly correct to view the work to grow WSL attendances as a long-term project. Each season so far – since the foundation of the league in 2011 – has seen a substantial growth in regular fans. Overall, WSL1 clubs experienced a 48 per cent increase in attendances for the 2015 season; the FA's figures indicated that the average match attracted 1,076 compared to 728 in 2014.

Gavin Makel, head of women's football at Manchester City, was thoughtful about the impact of the Women's World Cup, observing then that there wasn't the same kind of tribalism as was found in the men's game; fans of women's football were happy to watch any team rather than obsessing over one particular club.

'Women's football is more like how men's football used to be – you can get close to the players, get a photograph and an autograph, there's a nice atmosphere. People see it as a genuine sport,' he said in the summer of 2015.

Yet WSL2 clubs didn't have quite the same boost; they didn't get the same media coverage and they'd lost their only big name.

'We do as much as we can to raise the profile of WSL2, but naturally the broadcasters want to focus on WSL1,' admitted the FA's Katie Brazier.

'It just doesn't have the visibility of WSL1, and that's a shame,' said one fan of a WSL2 club, 'because if people in towns like Oxford, Durham, Reading and Watford were more aware of the fact that they have local clubs in the WSL structure, they'd be more likely to go along and watch them – especially with the post-World Cup publicity for the women's game generally. It feels like a struggle for WSL2 clubs to publicise themselves as being part of the WSL structure and it would help if the media just paid a bit more attention.'

Some fans of WSL2 clubs have wondered if they would have been better off staying in the Women's Premier League, a competition which runs through the winter – parallel with the men's leagues – and the gulf between the best and the rest is, perhaps, not quite so apparent.

'The [WSL2] sides who have previously played in the top division are very much better than most of the others,' says one Oxford fan. 'Their technique is better, their fitness is better, and they have strength in depth. Teams like Oxford are really enjoyable to watch – especially when they are showing a noticeable improvement from last season – but they struggle to field 11 players of real quality every week. Sides like Doncaster always look accomplished – and when WSL2 sides play WSL1 teams in the Continental Cup, the difference is even more marked.'

The Continental Cup is organised on a regional basis, and at this point it saw WSL1 and WSL2 clubs playing against each other in a mini-league format before progressing to the knockout stages. The FA is keen to point out the advantages of this – and again the rise in numbers going to watch these matches.

'The average attendance for the first round of those fixtures was 74 per cent up on last season,' says Brazier. What she did not add was the chasm in standards on show between the two top tiers of domestic football. WSL1's Arsenal beat WSL2's Watford 3-0 a fortnight after the end of the World Cup. Six days later, WSL1's Manchester City beat WSL2's Durham 5-0, and on the same night WSL1's Sunderland beat WSL2's Everton 5-2.

There were also some entertaining all-WSL1 games, of course, which flew in the face of recent form. Group One's London rivals Chelsea and Arsenal duked it out at Wheatsheaf Park, Staines, in mid-August; though the FA Women's Cup winners were also at the top of WSL1, and former mega-powers the Gunners had struggled in the league, it was the visitors who dominated the game, ending up 2-0 winners.

Chelsea winger Gemma Davison couldn't play against her former club as she was serving a one-match suspension after receiving a red card for a second bookable offence against Birmingham City the week before. Throughout the first half, fans in the main stand would have seen her stalking up and down the steps and rows; those a little closer to her would have heard her muttering, 'I can't watch this, I need to play.'

Chelsea certainly felt her absence. Despite her sparkling displays, she had not made the cut for the England World Cup squad; that seemed to give her an increased impetus to improve her performances even more. The cup winners also noticed the loss of Katie Chapman during the first half, injuring herself in a challenge and departing the ground on crutches.

Arsenal, however, did not subsequently have an easy route through the competition despite beating the league leaders. Their quarter-final match ended up being delayed for a fortnight while the FA investigated the possibility that opponents Manchester City had fielded an ineligible player in an earlier round. In what was possibly one of the most opaque and confusing FA decisions in WSL history, it ended up deciding that the charge had not been proven – although the FA did not have the correct paperwork filed in its office, City had shown e-mails that indicated that the right forms had indeed been received by the governing body.

The match was quickly arranged for a Thursday evening at Arsenal's home ground in Borehamwood, causing City manager Nick Cushing to bluster that it was impossible to prepare a team to win at such short notice, perhaps failing to acknowledge that Pedro Martinez Losa, the Gunners' manager, was in exactly the same situation. City were defending a trophy they had won during the previous season but they could not get past Arsenal, who edged through with a single goal from Spanish striker Natalia. They continued their progress with a thumping 3-1 semi-final win over Birmingham City and made their fifth Continental Cup final in a row, winning it at Rotherham thanks to two goals from Jordan Nobbs plus one from American striker Chioma Ubogagu.

Manchester City still had a chance to pip Chelsea to the WSL1 title, though. They needed Sunderland to do them a favour – always a dangerous tactic – and take some points off Chelsea, who had a two-point cushion over second-placed City going into the final day.

It was always a long shot and Emma Hayes's team finished their season in impressive style, securing their league and cup double with a crushing 4-0 win over Sunderland. Even though Manchester City also won, beating Notts County 2-1, it was never going to be enough. City could console themselves with another broken record, however – this time attracting a new club high of 3,180 through the Academy Stadium turnstiles to see that last match of the season.

WSL2 also went down to the wire, with Reading pipping Doncaster Belles to the title on goal difference two weeks after the top flight drew to a close.

As the champagne corks popped for some and the regrouping and reassessment began elsewhere, though, the rest of the women's football pyramid was just beginning in earnest.

Apart from the two WSL divisions and their Continental Cup tournament, all of the other women's football competitions in England run on a winter calendar, the same as the men's leagues, and the same as the European club competitions. They begin in August, run through the winter, and end in the spring; that includes the FA Women's Cup, which the WSL clubs enter in a later round, after the New Year.

Now that the WSL is firmly established, there is promotion and relegation between the two divisions – but there is also promotion between WSL2 and the Women's Premier League …there is also promotion from the Women's Premier League to WSL2. At least, that is the theory Because of the way the WSL operates – clubs apply to take part, providing extensive business and marketing plans as supporting evidence, and are awarded time-limited licences to compete in the league – its long-term development and progress is currently rather unclear, at least to those from the outside, and so is the future of clubs outside the top flights. When a club secures promotion on the field, it must then meet some tough off-the-pitch requirements to prove it has a suitable set-up to take part in the new, more elite competition.

While the WSL's strategy for future expansion involves a club development fund for its members, those at Premier League level and below don't have access to the same resources. Concentrating on how the WSL elite will capitalise on England's World Cup success may pay off but it may also be rather short-sighted. It's clear that already the WSL has seen a boost in attendances, and with sensible planning those gates will grow; an elite proportion of their players are instantly recognisable media figures; the improved competition at the top of the game has made for a much better spectacle; and the improved club structures and facilities have combined to stop the talent drain seen so often a decade ago as young women opted to study overseas – usually in the USA – on a soccer scholarship, enabling them to play and gain a degree. The future of the Women's Super League – assuming all clubs turn fully professional much sooner rather than later – is reasonably bright.

Further down the pyramid, there are many more questions to be answered. If women's clubs are expected to have a formal tie with men's clubs, which is what seems to be transpiring, this could cause problems further down the line; just look at the number of once-giants who had funding pulled by their partner club when the men had a bad season, such as Charlton's legendary side. Premier League clubs looking for promotion to the big time have to manage their winter schedule, invest in their set-up, and prepare their facilities and the players for a summer league without the same kind of support as the WSL clubs receive. Women's football in England has a storied history; but the FA's governance of it started only two decades ago. Before that (and even after that), women's football was resolutely amateur; full professionalisation at the elite level, and preparing to extend that professionalisation downwards, is a slow process.

The world's first football club

THE snowfall in South Yorkshire was minimal but the temperature was low. Sheffield FC's development team were quickly casting their eyes around for a potential alternative venue if their Home of Football ground, in the hamlet of Dronfield, was suffering from the deep freeze.

General manager Helen Mitchell was at the ground early on Sunday morning, four hours before kick-off, testing the state of the pitch and brushing off the residual frost. Her mobile phone was never far from her hand as she texted, answered and made calls to ensure that everyone was fully up to date with the day's arrangements – teams, officials, ground staff and catering.

By 11am it was clear that the ice resting around the penalty areas was melting, and the pitch was soft enough to take players' boot studs. The club's training ground – one of Sheffield United's facilities – was not going to be called into action.

Mitchell continued with her preparation work – making sure that the neighbouring pub, owned by the club, was ready to cater for the teams post-match, distributing the matchday programmes, and sticking the corner flags in their places. At noon she started to wire up the stadium's PA system, slotting in the somewhat elderly compilation CDs that comprised the pre-match entertainment. As the visiting team and management arrived at the ground, she sprinted out to form the welcoming committee.

She is essentially the founder and lynchpin of Sheffield FC women's team. She took on the role of player-manager at Norton Ladies in 2002, and realised very quickly that a sounder infrastructure was needed if the club wanted to progress – or indeed simply stay in existence.

'The first year was fine, then in the summer the manager said, "I'm leaving, I've had enough," two weeks before the start of the season,' she recalled. 'The girls asked me if I'd take over the management. I'd never done anything like that before, I had no coaching qualifications. I'd been in charge of the university team, but other than that, I'd done nothing. So I said yes because we didn't have any other option.

'I did that for a year, and it was just really, really hard work. There was a small committee looking at finances and organising, so I got involved in that, obviously, and it became very clear that this was just a hand-to-mouth existence. We were going nowhere, we didn't have a fixed base, each year we were looking for somewhere different to play.

'We thought, "Right, let's affiliate with a men's team, that's probably the best." We can get a stable base, a bit of support, and we can get our name out there. We were an isolated team, not affiliated, there weren't other teams playing for that badge. So I rang the chairman here, completely out of the blue, and just said, "How do you feel about having a women's team?" He was like, "Right, yeah, that sounds interesting, let's meet up."

'So we did, and he said, "Your timing's brilliant because we are looking for a women's team." So our call was really timely. We put together a five-year plan, where we wanted to be, what it would bring to the club, that sort of thing. The board said yes, and that was it.'

Sheffield FC are the oldest football club in the world. They are, understandably, very proud and very vocal about that fact. Their club crest bears that slogan; their office boasts a magnificent memorabilia collection from 1857 onwards, including a series of three letters from then-FIFA president Sepp Blatter congratulating them on receiving the governing body's Centennial Order of Merit and also accepting the offer of membership at the club.

Blatter was not in evidence at the Home of Football on this November afternoon but there was a healthy scattering of fans, many of whom were family members of the players, plus the traditional and proverbial man and his dog, Sunderland Ladies' first-team manager Carlton Fairweather, and even some media interest from the Netherlands – not bad at all for a development team match on a freezing Sunday. Half an hour before kick-off, as the squads emerged on to the now-lush pitch for their warm-up, the sun suddenly burst through. The players' variety of woolly hats and thermal gloves were still very much required, though, as were the cups of tea being gratefully guzzled around the ground as the chill wind continued to blow.

Despite officially being part of the WSL set-up, having secured promotion to the Women's Super League 2 back in May following a dramatic play-off with Portsmouth Ladies, Sheffield FC had a tough latter half of 2015. That was simply because the WPL, adhering to the traditional winter season, finished with that play-off in May, and Sheffield essentially had a year to wait before their first team could get back in action again – the WSL's summer scheduling meant they had missed the 2015 season, and could only take their rightful place come March 2016.

'That game was possibly one of the most intense games I've ever played in my life,' recalled captain Carla Ward. 'There was so much emotion in it that it was just intense from the word go, to the point where when that goal went in

I don't think any of us had an ounce of energy left. It wasn't frantic – it was more mentally draining. Honestly, I felt for them. Our girls were celebrating after and I had a horrible feeling for them. I had a word with their skipper and I was just like, "Someone had to lose," but it was hard. The emotion that day was unreal. It was a difficult day – and the best day of my life so far.'

The promotion to the elite of the women's game was something that Mitchell never expected.

'I remember very clearly the chairman Richard asking me, "What's to stop you going to the top of the women's game?", which at the time was the Women's Premier League National Division, Arsenal and everyone, and I just laughed. Ability? Money? All the rest of it. And he was like, "So that's all? So it's achievable then?"'

Mitchell's Sheffield team, however, exceeded everyone's expectations, securing a string of promotions; but she never thought they would be able to move into the WSL, founded initially as a closed league with no promotion or relegation. When the WSL2 was added, Sheffield applied for entry, never expecting to even be considered due to the stiff competition from more well-known teams nearby.

'We'd only been in the Prem 18 months at that time, I thought we'd have no chance, but we just did it as an exercise, which we thought would be useful,' she said. 'We didn't expect it, mainly because of how juvenile we were and how young we were as a team, but also we were geographically close to teams that were really well established. We got good feedback from the application, we knew there were a few things lacking which we needed to get in place, and which we went away and worked on, and two years later we got the chance through promotion.'

That was after the FA announced that there would be one single promotion slot allowing a WPL side into WSL2. However, the WPL is still split into two regional divisions, meaning a play-off between the two winners to decide the national champions. Then there was the fact that even though Sheffield won their play-off against Portsmouth, they still needed to go through the formalities of being granted a licence to compete in WSL2, meaning a lot of paperwork. Mitchell had a lot to prepare, but captain Ward never had any concerns that their promotion would be rubber-stamped.

'All the girls know that off the pitch we're well looked after, so I don't think there was any doubt in players' minds,' she said. 'When we won that play-off, everyone was fully confident that we had done our job and they had done their job, so although Mitch was very much "we'll wait and see", we always knew. There was never any doubt – no doubt in my mind. Everything she does is done to an absolute tee. When it was confirmed, it was party time.'

'We've had quite a few meetings to just go through things,' said Mitchell. 'I found that quite difficult because everybody else has been in it for two years, and they forget what it was like at the start. Obviously for us it is the start, and a lot of those things that they've been through where they're at now they forget to tell you the basics. I've been having to ask hundreds of questions about basic, basic things, I feel like I'm just bugging them all the time. It's a very big change. On the pitch, we'll cope with that, that's fine; but off the pitch, the contracts, the marketing, matchday experience, crowd figures, how are you going to get yourself out there. It's a big change, and lots of things for us to get our heads round, but we're getting there slowly.'

With such a sizeable gap between the end of the WPL play-off and the start of the subsequent WSL season, some of the Sheffield players had temporarily moved to other WPL teams to stay match fit, while Ward was concentrating on gaining her UEFA B licence coaching qualifications by working with the development side plus the Sheffield University team and in local schools.

'I'm the only female on a 26-man course, but I don't mind that,' said Ward. 'I quite like being around the men anyway, because it tends to be a little bit more brutal and you know you're going to get told if need be. It's been good, to be honest, I've learnt a lot.'

That meant she was on the sidelines to watch the Sheffield development team trounced by the impressive Sunderland. Rachel Furness, the visitors' Northern Ireland international with a wealth of first-team experience, marshalled their play, opening the scoring with a fine lob of young goalkeeper Lauren Santoro. The sun continued to shine even as the rain began to fall in a sharp shower, with a huge, bright rainbow spreading over the pitch at the end of the first half; the second half began with a spell of decent Sheffield pressure but their opponents soaked it up, hitting them with a sucker punch from Tyler Dodds, and wrapping up the game shortly after the hour mark courtesy of Charlotte Potts. Sarah Jackson's rather poor penalty, which goalkeeper Grace Donnelly palmed on to the inside of the post, was a mere consolation for the hosts; as they pushed players further forward they left holes at the back. Furness and Dodds both notched again in the closing minutes with Maddie Hill adding a sixth seconds before the final whistle as the rain once again pattered down on to the pitch.

Throughout, Mitchell had been poised on the stairs to the offices leading to the pitch, that ever-present phone still in evidence, as she assumed control of the team's Twitter account, posting regular updates from the game.

'Murdered,' she muttered at the end. 'Just not turned up today, just didn't get started.'

The players and staff shook hands after the match in the traditional show of respect. After a debrief and a shower, both sides headed off to the pub for their post-match meal.

It had been a busy week for Sheffield. Mick Mulhern – whose track record at Sunderland had made his name in women's football – had been appointed as the women's first-team coach prior to their entry to WSL2, officially replacing Mitchell for the 2016 season.

'I haven't got my UEFA A Licence, which is one of the criteria for managers, but I'd been thinking about stepping away for a few years,' admitted Mitchell. 'I felt I wasn't giving the focus the team needed, so I was quite happy, once I'd got my head round it, to step away, and it's been good for me to have a different focus.'

'When Mick came in, I was delighted anyway,' said Ward, 'but I was happy because I said to Mitch a long time ago, "What about Mick Mulhern?" She was like, "Don't be silly, he wouldn't come to us." In terms of where he is in the coaching world it's good for me individually, I can learn a lot from him. I ask a million questions.'

Both were honest that there had been some apprehension among the players about the new appointment simply because of a fear of such a big change.

'There's never been another manager at the club,' Mitchell pointed out. 'They all signed on the basis that I was the manager, and I think that's really hard then. Some of them have been here a long time and got very used to the way that I do things, but they trust me and they trust my judgement. I was very keen to bring someone in who wasn't going to change everything straight away, and that's something Mick and I have talked about a lot. We've got a good team here, they want to be given the chance, we've got to invest in them because they've got us where we are now, and he's done that at Sunderland when they came out the Prem. They've met him now, they met him this week, and it's all happened very, very quickly in the end, but they're pretty excited about it because they know his reputation and what he's done at Sunderland.

'He wouldn't be a popular manager if he didn't know how to treat people, and that's the big thing for them – does he know how to manage a women's team? It has its own challenges, but it's massively important to manage the group and get the best out of them.'

'Mitch is not going anywhere, she's the general manager, so not much will change in that respect,' agreed Ward. 'As a player I'm dead excited, we couldn't have got anyone better in for us to go on to the next level. A lot of teams go in to WSL2 to hold their own. I said to Mick that I am quite ambitious as a person. I've said to Mitch over the years, "We can go into this league and win it," and she'd always laugh at me, but we've got the quality to do it. Some of our girls have turned down WSL1 moves this year, and I said to Mick straight away, "Do you know what? We bring the right players in, we can go and win it in our first season." He had a little smile to me, and I said, "I'm not expecting you to agree or disagree because you haven't seen the girls and whatnot, but we're good enough." With Mick coming in, it's that name now to attract players.

'It is different for some people. Some people don't like change. Some people aren't looking forward to it, but to be honest with you a bit of competition will do you good. For me, I can't wait for a bit of competition. It's going to bring out the best in all the girls. It's exciting times, I think.'

On Mulhern's appointment, Mitchell assumed the title 'general manager', meaning many of her duties would stay the same, just without overarching responsibility for the first-team coaching and selection. Like many in the women's football pyramid, she had worked scores of hours every week without the expectation of financial recompense, simply for the love of the game, balancing coaching and management with her work as a landscape architect in a local practice.

With Sheffield's formal entry into a semi-professional league, though, she had reduced her hours at work to officially take on the part-time job of the women's team's general manager.

'When you've been doing the same things for 12 years, it can become a bit of a treadmill,' said Mitchell. 'It's been brilliant to have a different focus and a different challenge for me has been really refreshing, I've enjoyed that. We knew the sort of person we wanted to bring in, but it was just could we get who we wanted. It's been a big surprise, but it's exactly what we need.'

Ward, meanwhile, had her eye on the future.

'I want Mick's job in a few years,' she said. 'I've made no secret, to the chairman, to Mitch, "Look, one day down the line I don't see myself at any other club, this is where my heart is, and I want it, I'd love to do it."

'When I've been at other clubs, they bring in players as and when you need them. This club, you have to bring the right type of person into this club, and it's very much more of a family unit. Everyone looks after each other. It's not just about the football, it's about the group collectively, and it's different. I love it.'

Even though she was racking up the hours for her UEFA B licence, she was still recovering from a second spinal operation, undergoing regular specialised physiotherapy.

'I'm doing all right,' she mused. 'It's not that I don't listen but I've always rushed back before; I just hate being on the sidelines. This time round I've done everything down to an absolute tee and I feel really good. There are certain things I still struggle to do, it's horrible. Back rehab is the worst.'

Had she ever considered retiring? She considered.

'Everybody was saying, "You're going to have to retire, it's your back, it's not good,"' she recalled. 'To be honest six months ago after I did it again I made the decision in my head. Then as soon as I started doing rehab, I started thinking, "I can't. I can't give it up."'

An ironic smile crept over her face, and she glanced at Mitchell, who had just run past to riffle through some paperwork.

'Think I'll ever retire, gaff?' Ward asked.

'We'd have to cut your legs off first,' came the reply.

From Sweden
to Leyton

IT was a bright, sunny Sunday afternoon in east London the day after the clocks went back. Families with small children, wrapped up warm against the chill breeze, wandered through Mile End Park; groups of friends laughed and chattered as they rode their bikes along the dedicated cycle tracks.

In the middle of the green is a big leisure centre, housed in two buildings; fenced off between the two is an athletics track with a full-size grass football pitch in the middle, framed on one side by a stand of bleachers. This is the grandly-titled Mile End Stadium, the home of Leyton Orient Women.

There is plenty of space for spectators, although the track keeps them at a distance from the players, and on this October afternoon there was merely a scattering of interested folk around the vast perimeter there to see them take on Eastbourne Town in the London and South-East Regional Women's Premier Division.

The dugouts, situated opposite the stand with the bleacher seating, were unpleasantly close to the leisure centre's overflowing commercial waste bins; one could only presume that they were expecting a collection first thing on Monday morning.

Orient had been on a poor run of form, and watching them against Eastbourne Town you could see signs as to why. That is no disrespect to Orient; their group of players was clearly highly skilful, but their finishing left much to be desired. The problem was exacerbated by both teams getting increasingly irritated by offside calls – both clubs had provided an assistant referee each, and both were quick to lift their flags, sometimes correctly, sometimes wrongly, just as at any level of football.

Eastbourne took an early lead but Orient fought back with two well-taken goals before half-time. As the sun began to set and the shadows grew longer, the hosts became edgier. The substitutes, the substituted and the squad staff shouted encouragement from the sidelines, 'Lock this up!' 'We're winning this, they're tired now!' It was only when they scored a third and final goal – a spectacular strike from the edge of the box courtesy of Sophie Le Marchand – that they seemed to really believe they had the game won.

Thus they secured their second league win of the season, with only a draw on the board to add to their points tally – not particularly impressive for a club with serious intentions to win promotion to the Women's Premier League.

'We've not had the greatest start in terms of results,' admitted coach Chris Brayford, 'but we have had good performances. I know we didn't finish the chances, but in terms of penetration and the creativity, it's good. The quality is there to win – we need to go on a run of wins and find the consistency. The goal is if not promotion this season then to put everything in place so that we win promotion to the WPL next season.'

It is only a matter of months since the club took on the Leyton Orient name. Previously, they had been known as Kikk – meaning 'Kick In Kulan I Krysset', the Swedish colloquialism for scoring in the top corner of the net. Founded in 2004 by Andrea Berg and Karin Revelj, Kikk secured their stadium facility and welcomed players from all over the world to join their team. In 2011/12, they were champions of the First Division in their second season in the London and South East Women's Regional League. Now in the Premier Division of the Regional League, taking on the Orient name is a platform for them to begin to push on towards securing promotion to the Women's Premier League.

'When the club was founded it was founded by a group of Swedish women; it was their baby, the sponsors were a Swedish restaurant,' explained one long-serving player. 'Now a lot of them have gone home or stopped playing. It got to the point where there was such a disconnect with the name, the acronym, the spelling; when you start playing at a higher level, if you don't explain the Swedish thing, it sounds like Kick – so juvenile. Or you explain the Swedish thing and it just gets complicated! We never said the name. So giving us a name that we can say and identifies us to an area, a name we can say and people recognise – just the name change has been a motivation for a lot of people, in a way that's something to be proud of, something you can tell people.'

'WPL is a realistic goal,' said Brayford. 'We do need to plot what the appreciable improvements and developments are in each year. We've done a little bit of that. Really it was slightly frustrating in previous years – we've had the team to win promotion, but we haven't had the squad. The problem for us is the reserve team is a recent development, and that was a work in progress. We lost players because they were keen to play for the first team but felt there was too much of a gap to the development team, so if they weren't getting games in the first team they'd rather go to a division in between. We're in a slightly better position now. The Orient thing will help with this. People will see the development team as a path to get into the first team, which is how it's supposed to be.'

It was Brayford who approached Leyton Orient and asked to affiliate with the club, who had a women's team around the turn of the millennium but which folded in 2005. He met with the chairman, the chief operating officer and commercial executives to discuss the potential mutual benefits of Kikk rebranding as Leyton Orient Women.

'We didn't ask them for any contribution towards our running costs – just their support, particularly from an infrastructure perspective,' he explained. 'If we can get promoted to the WPL, there's funding available then, so as we go forward we hope to build the relationship, and they can see these guys are good on the pitch, they're well run, and they can increase the support. Orient have fantastic fans, a fantastic base, there's a real connection there. It's a good lift for everyone. Certain things have a psychological impact, and I think this is one of them, it's positive for the team.'

A compliance officer in the City by trade, Brayford has been involved with Kikk since 2009. He and the team felt that 2015 was the right time to think about the club's future development, after many of the founder members had moved on.

'It's something we've been mulling over individually and collectively for a while,' he said. 'Last season was quite tough. We've got a lot of good players, but we lost a couple of the best to a higher league, and last season we also had a lot of injuries, and we don't really have a lot of infrastructure or a lot of depth behind us. The Kikk thing had slightly gone away a little bit – all of the originals had gone, there were only a few players with that continuity. We were very proud of the fact that we'd got to where we were, and now it's time to push on.'

Of course, as with any club below the very highest of elites, there are also other off-field responsibilities for Brayford. The liaison with Orient was one of them – and the usual paperwork is another.

'Football admin, it's the worst, it can be so tedious and bureaucratic,' he admitted. 'Over the years we've got fines for some things and we want to scream, but people do chip in and help. There are people who want to help with things, but they have busy jobs – we have an A&E doctor, a newly qualified lawyer, quite a few teachers, all tough jobs in terms of constraints on their time, so it's tough to say to them, "Can you do this?" Like anything, you get the benefit of experience; now I can do it reasonably quickly. I've done a lot of coaching qualifications, that's my interest, that's my love; the admin is just to keep the club running. If someone ever takes that over, trust me, I won't miss it!'

Brayford began to coach girls' and women's teams after spending time working in the USA.

'One of the things that's said that I think is very true is that with the lads, it's a different engagement,' he said. 'You're constantly showing them that you're a better player than them, and that's fine, until they get to a certain age. With the girls, there's no competitive edge. They're interested in how you can help them, can you coach, do you have useful information to impart, and are you bothered about their progress.'

Orient's training takes place once a week on the 3G pitches on Stepney Green, under the floodlights for two hours on a Wednesday evening. The session after the win over Eastbourne was a chilly autumnal night; the squad arrived and slung their kit bags on the damp turf around the sidelines. They began the warm-up on time and by 8.30pm those players with the long days and heavy work responsibilities – or just a longer commute – began to trickle in and join the practice.

Some of the squad's current players had begun their careers at Leyton Orient's Centre of Excellence as children, and have been thrilled to see the wheel turn full circle and become Leyton Orient players once more.

'I was kicking a ball since I can remember,' said Lydia Cooper. 'When I was young, girls didn't play football. I actually started playing tennis for a tennis club because my parents said, "Look, you can't play football." They tried. My dad even took me down to Ridgeway Rovers but they said, "No, we don't take girls," so I just thought that was it. I'd play in the playground with the boys at school and I was on the school team. It was actually at a tournament with primary school that Leyton Orient were there, and that's when they saw me all those years ago, and then the rest is history. Tennis got booted out, and that was it.'

Lydia joined the Leyton Orient youth set-up as a nine-year-old and stayed there until she was 16, when she went to boarding school and then travelled for a while before moving to university.

'When I came back from uni the [Leyton Orient] women's team had folded,' she said. 'A lot of the girls I used to play with, they'd joined Leyton, so I went to play for Leyton FC for a couple of years, then *they* folded, and that's how I ended up here. I'm really excited to be an Orient player again. It's like going full circle.'

One of her team-mates, Connie Montiel-McCann, started playing for the Centre of Excellence at the age of 12 but found herself a little lost once she was slightly older.

'There were two Leyton Orients, really,' she recalled. 'There was the Sunday team and the idea was that it would feed in to the women's team. Then there was the Centre of Excellence, that was the more top-end stuff; we were playing against Arsenal, Millwall, who were the team at the time. When we got to 16, as far as the Centre of Excellence was concerned, that was it.'

After making the choice to play football as a child, she found the fun seeping out of the game during her Centre of Excellence years.

'On Saturdays when I was doing the Centre of Excellence, I wasn't playing very much, and I was never really told why I wasn't playing – I was just dropped and that was it for the season,' she said. 'The Sundays were always the same group of girls, who were much louder than me actually. I was very quiet. The Sundays were more enjoyable, I guess, but even with that, I was very ready to leave the whole Leyton Orient set-up. The Saturdays and Sundays at Leyton Orient, when I look back, were good, but they were really quite intensive.'

Connie kept playing while she was at university in Hull but more for the social side of the game, making good friends to whom she is still close. She also took time out to travel the world, spending time coaching at a camp in the United States, but chose that more as a straightforward way to see the country rather than because she wanted to be involved in the sport. On her return to London in 2012, she signed up for teacher training – and for Kikk.

'Every season I think it's going to be my last season,' she admitted. 'It's a really nice atmosphere. I don't know, it brings out the nicer or the best side of people, or maybe it just attracts nice people. Maybe a bit of both. I think I want my weekends back, I don't want to be running around in the mud and the rain – but I do still like it when I get there.'

Lydia, contrastingly, hated the thought of hanging up her boots.

'Really the only time I stopped playing was at boarding school and that was because they didn't do girls' football there,' she said. 'I tried to get it off the ground but nobody was interested. They were more into hockey and netball. That was only two years, but I've never not wanted to play football. I don't know when I'll give up. I've been out injured for eight weeks and it felt like forever. I hate not playing. I'm the worst injured person. I tore a ligament in my knee, and I'm just coming back now.'

She indicated her right knee, encased in a bright blue support. After weeks of painful physio she had just been signed off. Although she had been back in light training, she had been under strict instructions to avoid the risks of contact – but she had since received the green light to test out her full range of football skills. As she joined the training exercise, she shouted happily to her team-mates, 'You can tackle me now! It's fine!'

Most of the squad were sporting training kit announcing their supporting allegiances, or their place of university study. A handful were still wearing their tracksuits with the old Kikk logo – the new Leyton Orient kit was not yet available for either matchdays or training.

'It'll be better when we finally get our Orient kit,' Lydia announced. 'I don't think anyone feels quite like an Orient player yet – I think that makes a big difference, we're still running around in yellow and green and looking like Norwich. Once we get that it'll be a lot better.'

※ ※ ※ ※ ※

Three weeks later, the shooting practice had obviously been paying off. In their previous three games Orient had scored 19 goals, including ten against Aylesford, and six more against Eastbourne away to add to the three they had scored against them at home.

'The signs were all there,' reflected Brayford. 'The 10-0 was a big boost for them because in the game before, we beat Eastbourne, and we could have scored more goals, whereas in the 10-0 they really were great from the off. Sometimes it just needs that little bit of confidence. Sometimes it's shooting practice, sometimes it's repetition of basic technique, which they've all got brilliantly, but it's about building that confidence. It's good for a striker to go in to a game thinking, "You know what, I feel good."'

With any team adopting an attacking philosophy, the danger is always that the defence will be left exposed, but Orient were avoiding those pitfalls.

The fireworks were still shooting into the Stepney night sky – some celebrating Diwali, some left over from Bonfire Night – making a high-spirited training session something of a carnival.

'You definitely see it, how well they get on, and that helps us in terms of when things go wrong, they don't get on each other,' said Brayford. 'That makes a big difference. I think that means the players have genuine pleasure in others' success. That's what has to happen. You can't just think, "Oh, great for me" – you have to think from a team perspective.'

After the Eastbourne game, Brayford had treated his players to fish and chips for the minibus ride home; not as an incentive to win or reward, just as a token to mark their hard work. He was happy to dig into his pocket, but was not altogether approving of some of the more unusual orders.

'There were some controversial orders,' he recalled. 'I'm a traditionalist – my mum and dad come from the coast – and the idea of going to a fish and chip shop and ordering saveloy – it should be cod and chips.'

He already had a plan for the next seaside trip. 'Next time we'll have a less democratic approach. I'm going to bar certain orders,' he declared, then laughed. 'I may not. This may cause riots.'

On a more serious note, travelling to away games out of London can take up a good proportion of the squad's weekend. Fish and chips on the minibus home is a tempting addition to make that journey a little bit more bearable.

'Sometimes for away trips you might have a couple of people who have certain injuries that might not heal because it's so far, and it might have for a home game,' said Brayford, adding with a certain amount of pleasure, 'Because the spirit's so good here, we don't see it.'

Two new recruits arrived for training, and were immediately grabbed by Olympia Diamond, known to all as Oly, the new player liaison rep, who introduced them to the rest of the squad. The atmosphere at a training session will always be reasonably good when a team is on such an excellent run of form, but the Leyton Orient women pride themselves not just on enjoying their football but enjoying the social aspects of the game. There had been much discussion over which pair had actually won the recent pool tournament.

'I found out I was really bad at pool,' she admitted. 'It wasn't the first time I've played, but I thought I was better than I was.'

She laughed uproariously at that. Was it perhaps the famed beer goggles that had given her a false indication of her pool table skills?

'Maybe!'

Post-match socialising was also on the up, as Oly explained, 'We've done a Nando's after a game, which was good – there wasn't a ton [of us], because we'd lost, but it was good that we did it. People go to the pub, which we didn't used to do – after our game, we'll go and watch a match [on the big screens]. This year it's been good, people have wanted to hang out and be a bit more friendly outside the pitch.'

It was particularly pleasing for Oly, who had chosen to join Orient's previous incarnation because of the friendly atmosphere that was evident.

'I came to watch them play before I joined, just to see them interact, and that was a thing – that everyone seemed nice,' she explained.

It was making Brayford's job easier too.

'Even if we're buzzing from a victory, I always deliberately don't go to things like that – and it's not that I don't like Nando's!' he grinned. 'The players should be together thinking, "Yeah, we did brilliantly." They solve the problems. It's to their credit that we won the games. It's because of them. When they're more comfortable with each other, they're more able to talk to each other, encourage on the pitch, or make suggestions. It's all much easier to say to someone you've got a good relationship with. If you don't know them, you might be concerned or worried they may be offended.'

He grew thoughtful, clearly considering the team dynamic.

'I think from a team perspective, as a manager you've got to be aware of how they fit together,' he reflected. 'That's the alchemy of football. Nobody would ever be part of football if the best 11 players always won. There's an art in the team and how the team fits together.'

He glanced over to Oly, making sure she could not overhear him.

'Take Oly. Now, Oly is a fantastic player. She gives us a lot defensively, you find her dropping in to defend, even though she prefers a little bit being forward. She would never complain about that, she always does an amazing job, she'll do her best in defence, and that's because she has a fantastic attitude. If the team can see how things are working and helping each of them, that has an effect as well, rather than some feel that they're making a sacrifice while others aren't, which can really frustrate them.'

As the score of players began their warm-up under the floodlights, a figure slipped out of the adjacent cabins, clad all in black. It was team captain Danni Griffiths, a touch late for the session, running on to the pitch muttering, 'I'm always late for training.'

Danni had been called into a meeting in the office at 6pm, two hours before she was due to meet her team-mates and prepare for the coming weekend's game. Such factors do not impinge only on training but also matchdays; for every match Brayford faced the problem of juggling his first-team squad – some missing due to work commitments, others due to personal arrangements, others with injury and illness.

'For most of the games, the spine stays the same,' he said. 'The defence are confident that if they're under pressure the goalkeeper can deal with it. Because we're quite quick, quite positive, there will always be times when we may be facing overloads at the back, but if we're taking advantage from an attacking perspective, that makes it hard for teams. The defence are good and they don't give a lot up, and the midfield have been working really hard and protecting them well.'

He beamed

'It's been good!'

The buzz around training was the imminent arrival of their new kits in Leyton Orient colours – and their invitation to walk out at Brisbane Road during a men's first-team match to be presented to the crowd. Brayford was still working on signing up a kit sponsor for the women, but was hopeful that everything would be in place soon so that they could make the final switchover into being officially recognised as Leyton Orient Women.

'It makes a big difference,' he said. 'Anyone looking at the video of us now would think, "Well, which one's Orient?"'

The players were excited to visit Brisbane Road, but some added a note of caution to the glee.

'I am excited,' said Oly, with a hint of reluctance in her voice.

She paused.

'It was weird. At first I was like, "This is so cool," and then I found out that people here have done similar things. Danni, when she was at Colchester, they went out there after they'd been promoted, and they got a lot of sexist abuse. So then I got nervous. It's an exciting thing, and cool, but I am a bit nervous that we're going to get yelled at to get our tits out.'

Her face, usually wreathed in smiles, was serious. 'It's important to do it, to show that we're a presence. The first people will take the abuse, and then the people after us won't.'

Belles on the ball

DONCASTER Belles are probably the most famous club in English women's football. Their extensive history goes back to 1969 and the legend says that the then-Belle Vue Belles were originally formed by girls who were selling raffle tickets to the fans at Doncaster Rovers matches. This was long before the FA took over the running of women's football in England.

The Belles have historically operated fully independently of the men's side in Doncaster, despite a successful ongoing working relationship with them. That long history has been steeped in success. They joined the National League, run by the Women's FA (a separate albeit affiliated organisation to the FA), in the 1991/92 season, and wrapped up a league and cup double without losing a game, completing another in 1993/94. Their captain Gillian Coultard led England and gained 119 international caps; Karen Walker, their centre-forward, spent 20 years with the club and scored 40 goals for England. The team's record-breaking feats lured the mainstream media, with a BBC TV documentary, *The Belles*, screened in January 1995, and Pete Davies's 2006 book *I Lost My Heart To The Belles* inspiring the successful television drama series *Playing the Field*.

The Belles were one of the founder members of the single-division WSL in 2011; but then the FA announced plans to restructure elite women's football into two divisions and asked all clubs interested in participating – including the clubs already in the WSL – to undergo an application process, which involved written submissions as well as an interview panel. In April 2013, it was revealed that Belles would be competing in WSL2 instead of WSL1; relegation in all but name. The FA said that Belles had encountered three major stumbling blocks: their use of the Keepmoat Stadium as third priority; their failure to produce a satisfactory commercial and marketing plan; and their intent for 11 per cent of turnover to go on paying players, which the FA did not think was enough bearing in mind their cap at the time was 40 per cent of turnover.

Despite vociferous fan and media reaction, and the Belles' immediate appeal against the decision, it was upheld and they took their place in WSL2 at the start of 2014. It took them two seasons of competition to secure promotion back to WSL1 – and as soon as they did, they proved they had dealt with the implications of amateurism and small-town mentality by announcing the most ambitious plans yet for the development of a women's football club in England – Project Phoenix.

They declared that they would build the first elite training facility in the UK to be used by a women's club, and a group of their players would be given full-time professional contracts – for the first time since the club was founded nearly half a century previously.

Plans were unveiled for a large facility near Bawtry, which would include five grass and artificial pitches, a physiotherapy room, dressing rooms, an indoor heated pool, ice baths, a gym, residential rooms and offices; and in a nod to their storied history, the centre was named the Belle Vue Belles, in honour of the original name and founding home.

Investor Carl Lygo said in a press statement at the project launch in October, 'We are building a long-term legacy for women's football in South Yorkshire which will ensure that the Belles can more than compete at the highest level. It will be a community resource for the development of grassroots women's football and coaches as well as supporting the elite game. I wanted to put something back into my hometown to help the name of Doncaster be recognised around the world as a leader in women's sport. The facility will enable the club to have its own standalone operation and they will never again have to face the threat of insolvency.'

Faye Lygo, Carl's solicitor wife and the club's chairperson, was delighted at the imminent commencement of the construction work.

'Project Phoenix has been there in terms of something we knew the club needed from the beginning,' she said. 'It was glaringly obvious to us there was a total lack of infrastructure; the girls had a nomadic lifestyle, going to one training [ground] to another, being bumped off time slots, it was always there – we needed our own things.'

The Lygos had become involved with the club following their effective demotion, feeling that their legal expertise would be able to make a difference. With the benefit of hindsight, Faye was less angry about the decision than perhaps she and the rest of the club had been a few years previously.

'The more I've got involved, while I still think it was a little harsh, the way they handled it, I can see the logic, I can see the reasoning behind what they did,' she reflected. 'In order to push women's football forward, they needed to make us be more professional than maybe we were capable of being at the time. I understand why they did it – I just think in hindsight it probably could have been dealt with slightly differently, in a way that wasn't so harsh.'

After the Lygos became involved, they looked at ways to move forward in the future, and wondered if the club's history had not developed into a bit of a hindrance.

'I think the club can slightly be blamed for trading on its history a little too much and needing to bring itself up to date,' said Faye. 'Now we look back at it, it's been a hard two years for a number of reasons, personnel, finances, organisation. However, we've now got to a position where we're stronger than ever, and we've now got a plan that will give the club long-term sustainability and an independence they didn't have before.'

Although Belles work closely with Doncaster Rovers men's club, they are not part of the same organisation, which is rather different to the set-up at some of the other elite clubs. Indeed, the FA's strategy for women's football encourages top teams to collaborate with men's clubs in order to share facilities, support systems and potentially gain funding.

'We have a great relationship with the Rovers, but we're not part of the Rovers – that doesn't mean to say we can't work cooperatively with them, because we do, but we're not under their umbrella,' explained Faye. 'Sometimes you're almost vulnerable to the whims of others, so we wanted to be able to create our own destiny to drive the game forward – I think you need your own possessions.

'What women's football lacks is infrastructure. A lot of the clubs don't have their own facilities, and a lot of them don't have the first call on facilities. They're bumped to evening [training] sessions – even some of the big clubs until recently had evening sessions because they had to fit around the men – and I think we need our own facilities. That's not just us, that's across the board. Until we get that, we're always going to be a bit nomadic and a bit reliant on other people.'

Lygo was also hoping that by the start of the 2016 season, there would be between six and ten full-time professional players on the Belles' books, but was a little reticent to talk too much about that until nearer the time.

'We'd love to be regarded as a professional club, but it might be that we can't do it this year and have to build up for next year,' she admitted. 'Even though some of them may be working, they have jobs that allow them to be fairly flexible through the week – I joke and say they're almost like three-quarter players.'

The Belles' intent was for that flexibility to be mirrored in the new facilities they were planning.

'If they want to stay over and train in the morning because they're working in the afternoon, they can do that kind of thing,' said Faye, 'because the facility is just going to be there for them to use, to fit around them – they don't have to fit around a hire time on the facility.'

Winter 2015

Lionesses back on the prowl

W HEN Mark Sampson named his England squad for the Women's World Cup, perhaps the most surprising omission was that of the tricky Chelsea winger Gemma Davison. She had been in and out of the set-up for months previously but ultimately failed to make the cut for Canada.

'Everything happens for a reason,' she reflected. 'If that wasn't my time, then it wasn't my time. I'm only in control of now, I won't dwell on what could have been. Maybe I needed that little kick to keep pushing on. I do feel like I've taken my game to another level this year, and I can't dwell, I've got to push and think about what's going on now.'

Still, missing out on a World Cup hurt her.

'Of course it was disappointing,' she admitted, 'but I feel like I was in a place where I did everything I could to get there. I started the season on form; I just set myself a target of scoring goals, being an influence in the team at Chelsea, and that's all I could control. I did feel that I achieved my targets – apart from the World Cup.'

Davison is much travelled. She began her career at Arsenal, which one senses she still considers her real home; but offered the opportunity to play professionally she was happy to head to the USA, where she refined her obvious skills. Her pace and her ability on the ball were honed and when she returned to England, she was a player simply unlike any other in the league. She began a second stint at Arsenal before moving to Liverpool and then to Chelsea, winning the WSL title with each of them. Her influence on each side played no small part in their successes, so her sadness at failing to make the England squad for Canada was understandable. As a professional footballer, though, she was pragmatic.

'Of course I'd have loved to have been part of it, but I'm watching my friends on the TV doing really good things and you can't knock that!' she said, putting a positive spin on it. 'I watched every single minute, behind them all the way, and they've come back and they've taken the game to another level. I think maturity-wise I've not taken a setback from not being picked, I've pushed on even more.'

Yet she was brought straight back into the squad as England embarked on their Euro 2017 qualification campaign a matter of weeks after the end of the World Cup, beginning with an 8-0 rout away to Estonia. Davison gives credit to her Chelsea manager: 'That's credit to Emma Hayes for keeping me in a good place and keeping me pushing.'

Davison has said multiple times that Hayes was the reason she signed for Chelsea, and her praise for her coach has continued to be impressively effusive.

'I knew if I went to play for her that she'd get the best out of me, and she has this year,' she said. 'She's a great coach, she's got a great coaching staff behind her that buy into all her philosophies. Everything I've said, I knew she'd get the best out of me because she knows me as a person, she knows how I work, she knows how I work psychologically, she knows what I need to improve in my game. I feel this is probably the most consistent season I've ever had, and I think a lot of it boils down to the fact that I feel really settled and I know how much she values me as a player. She's stuck by her word throughout my whole career, and I need to thank her a lot for everything she's done – but that goes for the whole coaching staff.'

Davison became an integral part of the England squads in the autumn of 2015. Traditionally, players have talked about the phone call they receive notifying them of their selection. Now it's a little more high-tech.

'Usually it's via e-mail,' said Davison. 'Mark Sampson's quite good at communicating with players. I had a phone call when I was called into the Estonia camp about what was expected of me, and he's good at communicating why you're going. I've thoroughly enjoyed the last two trips I've been on.'

One of those was to China, where England took on the hosts as well as Australia.

'I've never been to China before!' Davison enthused. 'That was an experience. To play against China, they're a really top-quality side. I was really impressed with the way they played football, and all the crowds that came to watch.'

England lost narrowly to China, 2-1, with a goal from Davison's club team-mate Eniola Aluko, but beat Australia 1-0 thanks to Izzy Christiansen's second-half strike. It was a decent enough return for a long journey and little time to acclimatise to the time-zone and the very different weather conditions.

'Even though the travel time was long, everyone put 100 per cent into it,' said Davison. 'England do everything they can to get you in the best shape possible, and the preparation is top-quality. We want to go on pushing to bigger and better things. The girls have done unbelievably this year, and we want to keep building on it.'

The next step was a friendly against Germany in Duisburg. England had beaten their old rivals for the first time during the World Cup but the memory of a humiliating defeat still stung; in November 2014, with much fanfare, England's women played at the new Wembley for the first time, selling all the tickets available, but they were outclassed 3-1 by Germany and the crushing dominance of star striker Celia Sasic. With that being the case, a 0-0 draw on their turf was a highly respectable result.

Then England finished the year with another Euro 2017 qualifier in a downpour at Bristol City's Ashton Gate. A Sunday afternoon fixture in dreadful weather at the end of November limited the attendance, but still attracted 13,000 people to see Jill Scott's goal prove the difference against Bosnia-Herzegovina.

Arsenal's centre-half Jemma Rose made her debut that day. 'It was a dream come true,' she recalled. 'I've always wanted to play for England, I've always wanted to represent my country.'

Rose had begun her career at Bristol Academy, so playing in that city made that day even more memorable.

'Bristol's got a big meaning for me as well,' she said. 'It's all for my grandad – the last game he watched me in was at Bristol, so for me and my family it was a really special day, and something I'll never forget.'

Christmas wishes

I T was a Christmas gift completely unexpected. The Great Britain Deaf Women's Football team had been tweeting regularly for days about the money they needed to raise in order to get to the 2016 Deaf World Cup in Italy. The £10,000 target they were looking to crowdfund was a drop in the ocean when compared to the giant budgets of elite men's football, or even the monies available to some women's squads.

However, the Deaf football teams are run by volunteers and receive no central funding. The players themselves fund their games and competitions – hence the need to run a social media campaign. Thanks to a retweet and £5,000 donation from Stoke and England goalkeeper Jack Butland, taking them more than halfway towards their goal, it soon leapt into the mainstream, with the BBC, *The Guardian*, *The Independent*, Sky Sports and Eurosport all covering the story.

Player and appeal manager Claire Stancliffe was thrown into a whirl she really was not expecting after years of scrabbling around for press coverage – and cash. A senior sports coach for Northamptonshire FA, neither media liaison nor public relations have been part of her day job, and she was suddenly dealing with the glare of the spotlight and dozens of journalists getting in touch. On top of that, she was also incredibly surprised by the sheer generosity of Butland's actions.

'I couldn't believe it and even had to ask my mum if I was seeing things – never in a million years did we expect to get a donation that big and by a professional footballer,' she recalled. 'It's not just the donation that amazed us, it was the media attention – just goes to show how amazing social media is for organisations like ourselves.'

They smashed their initial £10,000 target and the donations continued to march in, with a signed shirt from Arsenal and England's Kelly Smith raising an additional amount.

'Every person, involved from staff to players, gives up their own time and expenses to represent GB,' she explained. 'It is a massive financial burden and a struggle. I have been playing for GB since 2007 and I have spent well into five figures on training and competitions and so on. Thankfully I have been supported by a lot of people and companies. Now I am at the point where I'm struggling as asking the same people and companies for sponsorship doesn't get me very far – there's only so much they can give.'

When the squad committee sat down in November to discuss the possibility of making it to the Deaf World Cup, the general consensus was that they would not be able to go.

'When you take into account the costs of training camps, food, travel, kit, accommodation on top of international competitions, each year we need many thousands of pounds,' said Stancliffe. 'After every competition we are always back to square one: no funds and having to scrape whatever we can together. Our match kit is four or five years old and we don't have proper training kit. We don't have any corporate sponsorship; we approach places but aren't successful.'

So Stancliffe proposed a crowdfunding campaign, and volunteered to lead the project.

'To fund absolutely everything from training camps to the World Cup, we would need in the region of £30,000, and we had to make a decision on the World Cup by the end of

December 2015,' she said. 'Therefore I suggested launching an appeal to raise £10,000 in 30 days using crowdfunding. I had seen many clubs use this before and thought we have nothing to lose – plus as a player, I would do anything to get my team to a major tournament. Why should we have to miss out just because of money?'

Even once the initial target had been met, Stancliffe and her colleagues were already thinking ahead. The squad would be aiming for the 2017 Deaflympics – and would need money for that too. While their profile was high, they would be capitalising as much as possible.

'That is probably going to cost a very similar amount to Italy – so will we be back to square one again with no funds?' Stancliffe asked rhetorically. 'That's what we are trying to avoid if possible. Players should not have to focus on fundraising all the time. It's tiring and heartbreaking at times as you get to the point where you think, "I can't afford it, therefore I can't play for my country."'

Pleasingly, the rest of the women's football community rallied round. Chelsea and England striker Fran Kirby joined the squad at their first training session of 2016, which was featured on international news bulletins, raising more awareness of the Deaf squad's campaign. Again, it was Stancliffe's brainchild.

'I thought I would ask Fran Kirby as it would be a great boost for the players to see the support we have – plus we were training at Reading FC and I know that Fran was at Reading Women for a long time, so it made sense to ask her,' she explained. 'Our first training session of 2016 was fantastic. It's great to make a start on what should be an incredible journey.'

New year, same problems

I N the second week of the new year, the FA announced the appointment of Baroness Sue Campbell as head of women's football. Formerly chair of UK Sport, she had worked on increasing participation and achievement there, and would now be tasked with doing the same for football, taking up her role in March.

She had plenty of tasks awaiting her. The new FA WSL fixture list was released on Wednesday 27 January – and immediately the backlash began. It had already been announced that the Continental Cup, previously operating on a mini-league system across both divisions of the WSL with round-robin fixtures, would switch to a straight knockout competition. However, the biggest change was WSL1's increase to nine teams in 2016, a transitional step on the way to a ten-team division the year after, meaning that with every round of league fixtures, one team would be sitting it out. On the final day of the 2016 season, the fixture computer gave a day off to Manchester City – one of the teams likely to be in the mix at the top of the table.

'Expansion of the WSL1 is needed and I understand they wish to grow the league slowly to ensure it is financially sustainable,' said Laura Grubb, who regularly watches the London WSL teams. 'However, I disagree with them expanding it to nine teams and not ten. It doesn't feel right that Manchester City won't be playing on the final day of the season and it risks making a mockery of the league if the title race excitement is hampered because of it. It almost feels amateurish that the league has been put in this situation.'

For a league beginning in March and ending in October, there seemed to be a lot of gaps between scheduled home matches, even allowing for FA Cup and Continental Cup competitions.

'The first four league games for the Belles are spread over three months,' pointed out fan Glen Wilson, who edits the Doncaster fan site Popular Stand. 'Their first two home league games are two months apart. It's almost pointless trying to build any hype for the opening game as it's so long to the next one.'

Sylvain Jamet, a supporter of women's football who blogs for fan site Daily Cannon, was understanding about the reasons behind the scattergun approach to fixtures.

'It is very messy in term of scheduling but you would expect it to happen really with nine teams,' he pointed out. What he did highlight, however, was the space in the calendar that was a knock-on effect of the English teams being eliminated early on from the UEFA Women's Champions League – another competition that runs on the winter schedule.

'What people do not see is the FA dodged a bullet with Chelsea and Liverpool going out early – otherwise the fixture list would have looked like the M25,' he said. 'I mean, quarter-finals, semi-finals and the final – that's up to five more games to fit into an already crammed schedule.'

Jamet suggested that the problems clubs faced with fixtures, with some congested patches and then weeks free, were potentially also part of the cause for English clubs' failure in European club competition.

'I think it is a very complex schedule, to be honest,' he acknowledged. 'The FA has to take into account the international calendar with the UEFA Champions League, the Euro 2017 qualifiers, the Rio Olympics and FIFA national team windows [requiring no domestic games so that the coaches of the national teams have all their eligible players at their disposal]. Now, obviously the FA WSL is geared towards helping the England team with good effect, but in the six years since it started the FA has never managed to get a good schedule in order to fit the teams. There is a reason behind the English teams struggling in recent seasons in the Champions League. I know Birmingham went to the semi-finals a couple of seasons ago but they beat an English team [Arsenal] in the quarter-finals, otherwise they were likely to lose.'

Although the FA scheduling has to take into account international commitments as well as European club competition, what it does not currently seem to do is take into account the practicalities for fans who might wish to attend games.

'Away fans have been given many midweek games that are difficult to attend,' Jamet pointed out. 'Some of them finish after the last train home has gone.'

Dealing with fans is something the FA WSL does well on an individual basis, emphasising the accessibility of the game, ensuring cheap ticket prices, and encouraging families to attend.

'There's always lots going on at games for fans – particularly young fans – to feel engaged, entertained, part of something,' said Wilson, 'but in my view not enough thought is given to whether matches are scheduled at times at which fans – particularly away fans or exiled fans – can actually get to the games.'

There does tend to be an assumption that fans will not travel to away games in the FA WSL – there is no segregation between home and away fans at these matches, and so data on the number of travelling fans (or even neutral attendees) is not gathered.

Some fans have begun to feel that fans' experiences are not as important to the clubs or the governing body as they once were – perhaps not a problem unique to the women's game, but expressed in unique ways.

'The FA WSL's main selling point after the World Cup was that it is a family-friendly league, but this season doesn't have that feel to it due to the number of evening weekday matches,' said Grubb. 'They also don't keep the fans updated – and the FA WSL website is always behind on the latest news. I just feel that the FA WSL built on improving the women's game after the World Cup and fear that all that good work could be undone this season.'

There is also the fact that since its inception, the FA WSL has focused heavily on improving the media coverage of the women's game, with broadcast partners ESPN initially, then with BT Sport, and more recently with the BBC adding a regular magazine show to its coverage. This has meant that the WSL games might have been watched by a wider audience from the comfort of their living rooms, at a time convenient to them – in 2015, it was often a Sunday evening.

However pleasing those viewing figures might have been, this tweaking of kick-off times might not be particularly conducive to high attendances. Many of the WSL1 grounds are not especially accessible by public transport, and do not have regular train services nearby, meaning that a Sunday night fixture might mean a fan is forced into non-attendance. When TV schedules play havoc with men's football fixtures, compensations are often made – clubs put on free coaches, for example, or the train companies delay the last train. With the smaller numbers and lower profile of women's football, no similar accommodations are likely to be made.

'It's difficult to televise games on Sunday afternoons given the proliferation of Premier League matches, and

Sunday evenings are the only time that the women's game isn't competing for air time with the men's game,' said Tim Stillman, a regular contributor to an Arsenal fans' website. 'But Sunday evening kick-off times don't work for the WSL in terms of who comes through the turnstiles. It's a tricky choice and probably the single biggest challenge the WSL faces at the moment.'

Some might also suggest that a Sunday night fixture is unlikely to attract the family audience the FA WSL is so keen to grab on to – after all, children have to go to school on a Monday morning. The midweek evening fixtures create a similar problem.

'There are too many weekday fixtures,' declared Grubb. 'The FA say they want to create a family environment yet I don't think many parents will be wanting to take their children to an evening game on a school night. It also makes it difficult for fans who are at work or university and need to commute to the matches. Many teams play each other twice in quick succession: Chelsea play Liverpool twice within the first four WSL games, and also play Sunderland two times in a row – both Wednesday evening games, not making it easy for away fans to travel.'

At the time of the fixture list announcement, not all the TV games were confirmed, but it certainly appeared that some teams had puzzling schedules. Arsenal, for example, had six out of eight FA WSL home matches scheduled for a Sunday afternoon kick-off – but three-quarters of their WSL games would be played in the first five months of the season, with one league game per month from August onwards.

'This is just absurd,' said Jamet. Nevertheless, bearing in mind the huge number of postponements down the women's football pyramid over the Christmas period, a summer league does remain perhaps the most obvious choice for the elite leagues – it just needs some amendments to make it feasible for all stakeholders, fans included.

'I do prefer a summer season for the women's game,' admitted Grubb. 'There are fewer clashes with men's football, the weather is usually nicer which makes it more enjoyable to attend and I believe it is more appealing for people that don't usually attend games. If they are not fully committed to attending a game, good weather may just persuade them to go!'

'I love the summer season,' enthused Manchester City fan Rob McKay. 'I think the weather really helps with the appeal – although Widnes [where Everton and Liverpool share a ground] and City can be cold, and are real wind tunnels – but I just wish they didn't have the break in the middle of the season when there is no other football.'

'I think the summer season is a good idea in principle that hasn't really worked,' said Stillman. 'There are international tournaments in three out of every four summers [necessitating a mid-season break], so in reality, so few games are actually played in the summer months. There are men's international tournaments most summers now too; in reality, it's almost impossible to dodge the spectre of the men's game. Lots of people tell me that they are not opposed to watching women's football, but they just can't find time to watch both men's and women's football. This again is a huge challenge for the WSL – how do you compete in an already saturated market? There aren't easy answers.'

'There are no miracle solutions, just compromises to be made,' echoed Jamet. Of course, with a restricted number of elite full-time clubs with varying budgets, it can be difficult to establish where exactly those compromises should start. Fans of the WSL, however, have some ideas.

'They should have more weekend games with afternoon kick-offs and not have such long gaps between games,' suggested Laura Grubb. 'If the FA are concerned about financial stability, maybe they should get the teams to play each other three times – more games for players will help improve their technical ability and their fitness levels, making the game more exciting. The extra games would also bring in more revenue for the teams through ticket sales and merchandise and reduce the length of the gaps between matches for the teams. This would also benefit the national side: if they become better players, England will do better in major tournaments which will then generate more fans, the fans will then go to matches and the game continues to grow.'

Wilson, as a Doncaster fan familiar with the WSL2 set-up, had a drastic if practical idea, 'Abandon midweek games. There's pretty much no need for them when the leagues are so small, they're too late for school-age children to attend, they're hard for players, coaches and support staff to get to around day jobs, let alone supporters.'

'Largely I think the league has been blooded pretty well, strategically speaking,' mused Stillman. 'They've also been careful not to put the league too heavily into corporate hands, which has had disastrous effects in America, where private individuals or corporate avarice has dismantled leagues on a whim. The domestic scene needs more variety now and the Conti Cup is clearly struggling to provide a good balance there. The league has been right to grow slowly, but more teams will have to join in the future to sustain and grow interest.'

Stillman wondered if a revamp and restructure of the fixture list might pay off – not just for fans and clubs but to enable players to reach their potential.

'It's a short season and we are already seeing players going to American and Australian clubs on loan because they don't play for five months of the year,' he said. 'Condensing the season would make the schedule better, but in a nine-team league, it would also mean large periods without playing and that would result in talent migrating elsewhere. I can see the logic in turning the Continental Cup into a straight knockout given the lopsided contests between WSL1 and

WSL2 sides last year, but now a lot of squad/academy players are going to be denied games. The group phase structure at least guaranteed a set amount of matches for fringe players, who will probably look to the American college system more readily now. Until the league is ready to expand or more teams have their own stadiums, I'm not sure what else can be done at this stage.'

※ ※ ※ ※ ※

Kelly Simmons has been working at the FA for years, in a variety of roles. The problem of the elite women's fixture list was one that remained unsolved, and one that remained her responsibility as head of the national game. In her office at Wembley Stadium at the start of February she was happy to recap the arguments for and against the summer season – but as yet she had no answers.

The rumour had been that the WSL clubs had been lobbying for a change back to the winter season, but Simmons clarified that no decision had been made.

'Obviously we need to make the decision in collaboration with the clubs,' she said. 'It's early days. There are real challenges with the women's football calendar. How do we best schedule a league programme that supports the fans, scheduling around FIFA windows and major tournaments? Because it's an international league, it's not just about England as well, it's about whenever there's a FIFA window [when international friendlies or qualifiers would be played], there's challenges around that. There's big competition times like the Euros and the World Cup. Because still the majority play on grass, there needs to be a re-seeding break, so there's all sorts of challenges around *that*. Broadcasters are quite clear – they want a run of fixtures that make sense, they don't want to keep breaking all the time. We're just trying to think – what's a better schedule and a better way of running this?'

The summer season certainly has some advantages, but Simmons indicated that it had not been as successful in terms of numbers through the turnstiles as had been hoped.

'We put it in the summer to put it in the spotlight, but you live and learn, don't you? In the summer holidays the fan numbers go down because everyone's away, and actually now because there's so much football on television, there's not many days when we don't go up against men's football.'

One of the initial reasons for launching the WSL was to improve the England team, allowing for a more professional infrastructure and better resources for the squad. As such, the WSL calendar also needs to consider their requirements as a priority.

'We try and make sure we do everything we can to support Mark [Sampson] and the Lionesses, to give them the time they need, so there was a lot of time built in to give them preparation for the World Cup,' Simmons pointed out. Indeed, there was plenty of time allowed in 2015 for the England squad to prepare for the tournament; but there was little time allowed for them to recover before returning to domestic action. They landed at Heathrow on the Monday and the WSL fixtures resumed the following weekend. Most England players were, understandably, given the day off, appearing instead to collect congratulatory bouquets in an on-pitch presentation, and acknowledging the applause from crowds bolstered by fans who wanted to see the women they had been watching on the television for the past month.

As a general rule, though, Simmons was right to observe that in England, domestic football has to take a break when international fixtures are scheduled.

'Some countries play without their international players,' she said. 'We don't do that, I don't think culturally it would be accepted; people want to go and see the best players. But that's how other countries get around it. The States play a lot without the US players. Australia kicked off their Super

League, a very short season, all those months of preparation – then on the first game the Australian Federation took their players to a tournament. Club v country conflicts will kick off across the world in the women's game just as they have in the men's.'

One of the options Simmons was mulling over was the concept of a winter break – long discussed in men's football, but always rejected. English weather is so unreliable, of course, that scheduling the break around the bad weather would be near-impossible; and giving the players a festive fortnight off over Christmas and New Year would result in mutiny from fans who have traditionally enjoyed their Boxing Day and New Year's Day fixtures.

'If only we could predict when the rain will come!' she laughed. 'That's the problem. You'd say, "Okay, put that break in and rework, let's have that time to break for the players when it's the worst period of time weather-wise, when the games are off" – but that could be anything in our winters, it really could. So that's quite hard as well. Long-term you do wonder if most of the top games will be on synthetic, high-high-quality 3G, and then the weather won't be one of the factors you're trying to grapple with, with re-seeding.'

If the WSL switched back to a winter season, with or without a break, it would bring it back in line with the rest of the domestic pyramid, making promotion much easier rather than leaving a team like Sheffield waiting for almost a year before returning to action. Leaving the WSL as a summer season, disconnected from the rest of the clubs, also helps to reiterate that there is currently no relegation from the bottom of WSL2 back into the WPL. The WSL2 clubs have been awarded their licences until 2017, so are assured of their places in this closed system until then.

'Obviously we're committed to take the winner of the WPL, so another advantage of flipping the season would be being able to relegate and link the pyramids back up,' said

Simmons. 'You can't relegate out because you'd just fold the club. You can only promote for so long until we're full; especially the top tier, how many teams can you realistically have in that?'

Preparation for promotion – for those clubs in the WPL looking to make the step up – was supported by the FA.

'They run a promotion-ready workshop for the ones who think they are going to do well, because it's not for us to decide at the early stages who might come up, that would be far too political!' she said. 'They start to take the clubs through the criteria for the licence, and look at where there might be gaps and any support they might need.'

Although WSL2 was ostensibly semi-professional and the WPL amateur, the results in 2016 show very clearly that the gap between the two was rapidly closing, and part of that was down to support and funding from a men's club – very different from the previous set-up within women's football, where clubs ran themselves independently.

'Ultimately if you're Brighton, it'll be about supporting them with added cash to make sure they can meet the criteria of WSL2, but they've got a massive head start: they've got training at the academy, they're playing at Sussex County FA's ground, they've got a lot of support within the club, they've got a lot of infrastructure, they've got a fantastic head of women's football in there. They're the sort of club where you think they're probably not going to have that much difficulty meeting the criteria.

'It's harder for the clubs that haven't got those connections and partnerships with men's professional clubs,' she went on. 'Bristol Academy, one of our strongest clubs for a number of years, they've struggled, got relegated, and now they've just cemented a partnership with Bristol City. It's very hard for women's standalone clubs to compete at that level without any partners; if you go back to pre-WSL a lot of those clubs at the top were really grassroots football clubs. They were doing fantastic work, so in no way is that a criticism, but they were amateur players – as in non-contract, run by volunteers, pay and play, maybe a bit of money from a men's club, a bit of support, not an overly different financial model from a lot of our grassroots clubs – yet they were the elite, so that's the one thing that's changed so much in the last few years is the business model of the top clubs.'

Up-and-coming Brighton had recently thrashed WSL2 Oxford 10-0 in the FA Cup, causing some raised eyebrows around the women's football world. Oxford were, of course, in their off-season, but nevertheless that was a resounding result.

'I think there are some great clubs in the WPL – I haven't seen Oxford play for a little while but I'm not surprised about Brighton,' admitted Simmons. 'I went to watch Brighton play when they had their first game at the Amex [the men's ground], and I thought they were fantastic, great football, ambitious club, support right from the chief executive of the men's club right through the club, embedding women's football. The pyramid has got to allow for those ambitious clubs who do well on the pitch – and have got the right infrastructure around it – to come up. It's all about strengthening the league and strengthening the women's game, connecting the pyramid, you've got to keep those [routes] open, somehow, but it does need looking at as part of the new strategy coming out soon.'

Baroness Campbell would be overseeing that new strategy, Simmons explained, but she would not be in post until the middle of March. Simmons was obviously excited about the arrival of her new colleague, enthusing about her achievements in sport already, and expecting her to bring that experience to lead women's football into the future. Additionally, as she pointed out, Campbell and her team would be able to draw on the information gathered by the FA since the WSL's launch.

'We know a lot, lot more now,' said Simmons. 'We've got more resources, and we've got more human resources. When we wrote Gamechanger [the FA's five-year plan to improve women's football, published in 2012], it was really about trying to make sure we capitalised on 2012 [the Olympic Games] and come out with a strong message that we're serious. On the back of the Olympics, we'd already got the Super League in place, we still had to go and get the broadcast partners. We decided to separate the rights commercially and then get partners behind the women's game for the first time – we needed revenue to invest back into the game.'

She paused.

'I can say this because I wrote it,' she went on, smiling, 'but [Gamechanger] wasn't really a strategy, it was more like a commitment of things to do. There were certain areas of it where we just hadn't got people in place, so instead of, "This is our performance plan," it was like, "We need to appoint a performance lead," and, "Please give us some staff so we can do this." Obviously we've gone and done everything that we said we were going to do in there. We've expanded the WSL, delivered and sold a commercial brand, we've got two broadcast partners, created a brand-new elite unit at St George's Park et cetera, but I think this strategy will be different because the last one was almost about putting the foundations in place. This one will be more about making sure we've got strong connections right through the pathway to give ourselves the best chance to develop football and achieve elite success – really good clubs, thriving competition. There's more to play with, really.'

Because the WSL was an entirely new project, with an entirely new system of selecting participating clubs, it was difficult to set actual metrics for success, but the FA did have targets to meet.

'We had targets for participation, targets around fan numbers, commercial targets,' explained Simmons. 'We agreed that with the board. We were tracking a number of KPIs in that sense where we could. I think with this [strategy], there'll be more.'

Simmons was refreshingly pragmatic about the value of strategies in themselves, pointing out that they were no use at all without people to put them into practice.

'It comes down to quality of people at the end of the day, executing the strategy, because every sports strategy will want elite success, they'll want to have support for their equivalent of our Lionesses, and how do we develop talented young players, and what's the infrastructure of coaching, sports science, sports coaching, medicine, the professional infrastructure to support them to give them the best chance to excel in their sport, and how you're going to widen the base, the participation, how are you going to commercialise the game, what's your elite competition going to look like, and the fans – how do you knit those things together?' she explained.

'The quality is in the execution. As our chief exec said, you never read about strategy, do you, it's how well it's implemented. The work has started. We've embedded women's football across the division so I'm the strategic lead on the senior management team for women's football, but it's embedded across all the directors, who have got responsibility for it. Our commercial director leads on delivery of the women's commercial programme. The technical directors work across all of the England teams, men's and women's, so it's embedded. Sue's job will be to come in and have a really good look at it and drive the game on further in the next four or five years.'

Signing on

DONCASTER Belles announced a trio of big-name signings on New Year's Day. Former Liverpool stars Natasha Dowie, Becky Easton and Katrin Omarsdottir all put pen to paper, indicating the Belles' ambition in a more public and immediate way than their training facility plans could ever do.

Meanwhile, the other promoted side were making arrangements for the coming season in a far more low-key way. Reading had made a storming start to the 2015 season, primarily thanks to the impact of forward Fran Kirby. She had been WSL2's top scorer in 2014 when her team finished third; even following her departure Reading clung on tenaciously to top spot despite the pressure from Belles and their star striker Courtney Sweetman-Kirk.

Yet Reading's preparation for 2016 was nowhere near as attention-grabbing as that of their rivals – but it was equally important in its own way. They had spent the previous years playing their home games at the Rushmoor Community Stadium, in Farnborough, Hampshire – about 17 miles from the men's team's home ground, the Madejski Stadium, by junction 11 of the M4 motorway.

The improved stadium requirements – and the increased attendance targets – for WSL1 sides, however, meant that Farnborough was no longer an option for Reading. Instead, they announced a new home – Adams Park, Wycombe, Buckinghamshire, the home of Wycombe Wanderers, around 25 miles away from the Madejski and 35 miles away from Farnborough.

'It was a very tough decision to move from Rushmoor Community Stadium,' admitted Reading's general manager Jon Horton. 'We had built a great relationship with the matchday staff at Farnborough FC, we had also built a strong relationship with Rushmoor Borough Council and we were keen to work with both parties to help develop the ground and promote women's football further. Unfortunately, with our contract expiring and the licence requirements of WSL1, negotiations with the owner became unrealistic on a new agreement and we therefore had to look elsewhere.'

One of the quirks of the Women's Super League is its vast difference in organisation from traditional British football. Historically, clubs have sprouted up in local communities – perhaps from workplaces, or groups of friends – and the locality has remained an important part of clubs' characters. In recent years, stadia have been built in out-of-town locations, with clubs moving from their initial homes in residential areas simply because of the requirement for more space and better facilities, but proximity to the original community has remained vital. Luton Town fans protested vehemently when there were plans to move them two junctions north up the M1; the saga of Wimbledon's planned move to Milton Keynes and the eventual compromise of calling the newly-situated club 'MK Dons' led to accusations that this was simply 'franchise football' – something that is common in other countries, such as the USA, but anathema in British sport.

Yet this franchising – or as the regulations term it 'licensing' – has become an integral part of the WSL from the start. Ray Trew owned Lincoln Ladies and Notts County (the men's Football League club), and in 2013 announced that the following season the Ladies would be competing as Notts County Ladies instead. It meant the women's team relocating across the Midlands, away from their initial fanbase; but it also meant that they would have a firm, formal link with a men's club, which is something the FA has encouraged with their WSL teams. Although community work is important for all football clubs, WSL teams' home grounds are not necessarily a part of that; Arsenal play in Boreham Wood, Liverpool and Everton ground-share outside the city, and Reading have not been able to make a home in Berkshire.

Horton said the club were fully supportive of the move, but admitted that the response from their fans has been mixed, 'The fans we gained from the Farnborough area have lost out; however, we believe our fanbase will increase as Adams Park is more accessible to existing Reading FC supporters who previously found Farnborough too far and difficult to travel to via public transport and road. Initial season ticket sales are already up on 2015, so where we have lost a few fans we are already gaining others from the Reading and Wycombe areas.'

Reading already had a good working relationship with Wycombe, with the under-21 men playing five home fixtures there. They already knew that the ground was up to scratch for WSL purposes, as the Continental Cup Final and FA Women's Cup semi-final had previously been hosted there. It seemed a fairly straightforward decision in the end.

'It's a move that brings us back to our home county FA of Berks and Bucks, whereas previously the ground was located in Hampshire FA area – this allows us to work more closely with our "home" county FA to develop awareness and support within the county,' explained Horton. 'Wycombe Wanderers provided us with a very positive response to introducing women's football to Wycombe Wanderers fans and the area. They are enthusiastic to work with Reading Women FC to cross-promote and develop female football.'

The need to develop women's football in the area and attract a decent attendance was key. Doncaster and Reading had average attendance targets of 800 for the 2016 season, a swathe below the aim of 1,100 for all the existing teams, and an allowance made only for their initial season in the top flight. Before the season started, Reading had appointed a marketing officer to concentrate efforts on drawing crowds, and had already planned to work closely with Wycombe Wanderers during the season.

Their plans were clear and sensible, and yet the obvious questions had not been answered. Wycombe Wanderers already had a women's team. They played in Slough, not far from Reading. If Wycombe wanted to develop women's football in the county, couldn't they do so with the team that already bore their name? And what about Reading's men's club? Weren't they interested in promoting women's football in the area?

Wycombe Wanderers FC have had an intriguing recent history. Now owned and run by the supporters' trust, they have been focused simply on keeping their club alive in recent years; though supporting women's football would have been nice, they were working at maximum capacity just to keep the men's team afloat. One of the ways in which they brought in money was through renting their ground out to other teams, most recently and lengthily to Wasps rugby team.

'They'd been with us for going on 13 years, which was very beneficial to us in terms of the rental fees they paid to the club,' explained Wycombe's communications officer Matt Cecil. 'It made our stadium a much better visitor attraction; we had far more people coming to it week in week out, spending their money, so that worked out very well for the football club.

'When Wasps decided to leave in December 2014 and go to Coventry and bought their way out of the contract early on, it left a void, really. We've got this sporting facility, used

25 times a season for Wycombe Wanderers matches, but there was scope there to branch out and have more football on the pitch.'

Adams Park was already used for one-off matches, such as the Continental Cup Final in October 2014 and some Premier League under-21 matches, and for a handful of Reading men's youth team games.

'Whoever it might be that we're hosting, we get great feedback every time that we do it,' said Cecil. 'Word gets round, and we've had many more enquiries from other sports clubs who maybe want a one-off game or to look at a longer agreement, and we have to pick and choose what we can do, what's best for us, and for the pitch as well.

'When the approach came from Reading Women, the relationship with Reading's men's side was already there from the games that we'd hosted. It falls quite nicely that the games are over the summer so it's not too much burden on the pitch during the men's season. We were conscious when we hosted the Conti Cup Final of the way that women's football is going: matchdays being a much more family-friendly environment, it's much more about having a good day out rather than being grossly attached to the football. Obviously that is a big part of it as well, but in order to attract people down to the games there's a lot more to it – a lot more than we would put on for a men's game. The family entertainment there is quite limited; for the women it's much bigger and bolder, if you like.

'We're very happy to have them here. We want it to be a success, as they do, we want it to be a long-lasting relationship. It has benefits for us not just in terms of the financial side of things, but again highlighting Adams Park as being a sporting venue that people want to come to.'

The question there would be whether or not people wanted to go to Adams Park, Wycombe, to see a team under the Reading banner play football. Cecil was optimistic that Wycombe fans would take the new arrivals to their hearts.

'Our fanbase is quite significant,' explained Cecil. 'What we've seen from the under-21 games that we've hosted here, there is interest among Wycombe fans for coming along to other games at Adams Park. They enjoy local sport, whether it's Wycombe Wanderers or something else.'

That led to the development of a strategy with Reading, promoting their WSL games to the Wycombe fans, using the Wycombe website, social media and the matchday programme, as well as a presence in the local community, including a trophy tour around schools, and a stand in local shopping centres.

'We certainly don't see Reading Women as any competitor to us: the matchdays don't clash, and I don't really feel that we're fighting for the same audience either,' said Cecil. 'Price-wise the tickets aren't restrictive at Reading Women, so certainly it's not as if Reading are treading on our turf. It's great to have one of the more successful women's teams in English football coming to Wycombe Wanderers, coming to Adams Park.'

Was there a possibility that Reading as a brand could begin to encroach on territory that had long been established as Wycombe's? Cecil did not think so, certainly not at this point. He was honest also about Wycombe Wanderers' relationship with the women's team that shared their name: it had been neglected previously, but was good and improving all the time. He felt that having Reading playing WSL1 games at Adams Park did not tread on their toes either; the distance between the two teams' league status was simply too wide.

'Our chairman is very big on the brand of Wycombe Wanderers and who it represents, and who represents the brand,' he explained. 'They're on our radar, we'd like to integrate with them more as time goes on. We might not be ready yet as a club to integrate them at the moment – we're solely focused on penny-pinching and making sure that the club survives, we're not completely over the worst of it. In terms of making Wycombe Wanderers Ladies a successful operation, it is going to require investments of our time and funding and we just don't have the resource for it at the moment.

'We want to put them in the public eye a little bit for our supporters, recognise that there is a ladies' team out there, and I think a few of our fans have gone along to some of their games. It's not the highest level of football; hopefully they can continue their upward climb and get a little bit closer to the WSL structure, but at the moment they're not close enough to it.'

If they did climb higher up the pyramid, playing at Adams Park themselves could be a possibility.

'I think there were a few eyebrows raised among people close to our women's team when we accepted Reading coming here: why can't we do the same for Wycombe Wanderers?' admitted Cecil. 'But the harsh reality of it is if we were to host Wycombe Ladies here, the cost to us to open the ground up, it just wouldn't be viable; the pitch maintenance as well. We only have a certain amount of games here each year; if we were to host Wycombe Ladies would it come at the expense of Reading Women, who financially are a much better pull for us? If Wycombe Ladies were to get in a position where they were higher up the ladder of women's football, then I suppose there might be more reason to work more closely with them.'

They were the words of a pragmatist – so often necessary in the emotive world of professional football.

Money, money, money

BIRMINGHAM issued a statement at the start of January almost as an apology to their fans – the legendary Karen Carney had left the club for a final throw of the dice at the league champions Chelsea, and few signings seemed on the horizon.

Tim Andrews was announced as the club's new CEO after years of commercial sponsorship. Cheery at the start of his tenure, he had plenty to say about the potential of the Blues. He happily pointed out their strong history and their pride in their youth development scheme, but admitted that with the improved budgets at the top of WSL1 – he named Chelsea and Manchester City specifically – it could take a few years for his team to be competing for trophies again.

His manager David Parker agreed. 'If you look at the women's game and the money they're spending, business-wise it's absolutely ridiculous,' he said in February. 'It's like suicide. If anyone was to come from the outside world, you'd be shutting down the whole women's game overnight. That's the reality.'

He pointed out that women's teams were now effectively dependent on finance from their allied men's clubs, meaning they were also dependent on the men's on-pitch fortunes.

'The game doesn't make money, it makes very very little, and the players now, what they're demanding in terms of salary, welfare, infrastructure and facilities, it's just not comparable to reality,' added Parker. 'Over the next couple of years, there's going to be some serious revenue needing to be generated. People have got to think about that very carefully. The only saving grace around the corner is the TV rights, which is up for grabs in 2018, but that all depends on how it's negotiated and how that money is then redistributed to the clubs. That is the only way forward to make it sustainable.'

Even some of the bigger names in women's football had been taken by surprise by the cash injection from some clubs. At the WSL's inception there had been a strict squad cap and a wage cap; as the competition established itself budgets became rather less restrictive, and often benefited from funding coming from a WSL team's alliance with a men's professional club.

Arsenal captain Alex Scott had clearly lost patience when she spoke to *The Guardian* after the Women's World Cup, describing her frustration that the club were falling behind the likes of Manchester City and its integration of the men's and women's set-ups. She recounted the way that Arsenal's women's teams had to sit around in London Colney coffee shops, waiting to access the training facilities until after the men had left for the day.

'I was coming from a player's perspective,' she explained some months later. 'I wanted us to be challenging. I've been at Arsenal my whole life when we have been winning. I don't want to see my club fall off.'

She was pleased to report that progress was finally being made, although she stopped short of crediting it to her complaint in the media.

'Arsenal have invested,' she said. 'They've built our own little bit of the training ground, we are in every day now, and we are actual professionals, so there's no excuses, like we have done in the past. I think it's great. In terms of speculating about budgets, Arsenal run it as a structure like the men's team. We don't want for the league to go crazy and then close and we don't have a league. It's about every team being sensible and making sure the league is sustainable.'

One problem that several clubs reported – from WSL down to the better amateur teams – was the influx of agents into the women's game.

'All of a sudden after the World Cup, they've sprung out of nowhere,' said one WSL general manager.

'"Oh, you need to speak to my agent!" I don't need to speak to your agent, thank you very much,' said one administrator. 'It's coming on a bit too fast, I think – these youngsters especially with their agents.'

The value of an agent below the very top WSL1 players is admittedly limited; as one lower-league manager asked rhetorically, 'What are they going to bring you? They can't even do boot deals at this level. There's no potential earnings for these agents because there's no potential earnings for the girls at the moment.'

Even if players were not signed to agents, the commercial potential of the women's game had not passed them by. Their contract negotiations were increasingly revolving around money rather than career opportunities and the prospect of becoming a full-time professional footballer.

One administrator said that a transfer target had reported that she was more inclined to sign for another team because they were offering her marginally more money. Below the WSL1, where teams are semi-professional, mostly playing for expenses alongside a job working in the club, or resolutely amateur, the sums involved sound ridiculously tiny – but for young women looking for their first steps in the industry, a few pounds' difference in expenses can prove decisive.

'I don't want players like that,' said the administrator. 'Even if I *could* give her that and say, "Yeah, that's fine, we can give you this and give you this," I don't want players like that.'

This administrator's club chose instead to focus on developing young talent who were truly committed to the cause.

'There are players who have worked so hard, they wanted to do it, and they did whatever they could to make sure that football came first,' said the administrator. 'I've got some players who are asking for their month's expenses in the middle of the month. I don't need girls like that. I know that sounds awful. I'll give those opportunities to the youngsters and know that I've got a squad who wants to be here and will fight for each other.'

Yet that raised concerns within the club about their ability to protect promising young players under the age of 18, who could not be signed to contracts.

'We have years in which we can't contract a promising young player – if someone comes in and says, "Well, we can't offer you a contract but I'm going to give you all of this," how can I stop her?'

Many managers and administrators at different levels were concerned at how quickly the women's game was becoming commercialised and how easily players' heads were turned by promises of financial gain.

More than anything else, there was a fear that these sharp business practices and monetary demands would lead to a loss of women's football's unique qualities – specifically a love for the sport.

'It's not even about professionalism,' reflected one general manager. 'These players aren't even thinking, "I deserve it." They're thinking, "I want this stuff." They're saying, "Well, she's got an agent, so I think I need to get myself an agent, and get myself a better deal," and it's becoming about everything other than what they're doing on the pitch.'

A coach of an amateur side, who felt some of his players had been poached by a neighbouring club in a higher league, added, 'Players contact us; players speak to other players. That's okay. But there are clear rules about if you formally contact another club's players – you tell the club seven days in advance. There's more of it going on. It's frustrating. People try to give the false impression that women's football is different to men's football and they're all much better behaved. There are lots of things that women are better at, but there are still some dodgy characters.

'If a WSL team comes in for one of our players, it'd be hard to know what to say. A WPL team? Well, that's where we're trying to get to; especially one struggling, I think we can give them a game. But there's still a big divide [between the WSL teams and the rest of the pyramid]. They see that they've got the support and infrastructure – but it's wrong, the same way as it would be wrong if we did it to a third division team's best player and just gave her a ring.'

Faye Lygo, chairwoman of Doncaster Belles, agreed that the number of agents in the women's game was increasing.

'We spoke to the PFA just after the season finished and they were telling us how rules on agents have relaxed,' she said. 'Some of them are ridiculous – it was just ridiculous. Maybe they are familiar with the men's game, but obviously that's not the women's game. They were asking for fantastic amounts of money, benefits, all this sort of stuff, and you just think, "The women's game can't sustain this at the moment."'

Lygo wondered whether the high profile of the top England players and the decent salaries they were able to command was affecting the others competing in WSL1, and whether the new agents were expecting their clients to shoot straight to the top soon.

'I do think personally it's a bit early for agents to be so pushy, because it'll just drive up the wages in the big clubs and the middle clubs won't be able to compete,' she said. 'Even in the last two years it's changed phenomenally. More and more of the men's clubs, like Man United, will eventually get their own women's team, and then it will all turn into the men's game, it will just be a replica, because they'll have the money to just fund it. The development of the top teams is dependent on the benevolence of the men's club that they're associated with.'

The Belles, despite a good relationship with Doncaster Rovers, had retained their independence, in the face of the FA's encouragement to women's teams to align with men's clubs. As Lygo observed, the biggest and best WSL clubs were the ones most strongly supported by a men's club, making it harder for smaller, standalone clubs to succeed.

She was also concerned about the rate of professionalisation in the women's game, wondering if the pace of change was just a touch too much too soon.

'Actually, I would say it's a bit like recycling – the council force us to recycle, you only had a wheelie bin so you couldn't fit it all in if you didn't recycle, so now people recycle, and they don't think anything of it,' she said. 'So pushing us to professionalise is a good thing, and it's making us do it, but it's going at such a pace. We're still really dependent on volunteers but that can't go on forever.

'If we can get our message out, we can reach more people, but we haven't got the budget to run a big radio campaign or anything like that, so people don't always know and it's really hard to get that communication out. If you've got your own facilities and your own ground you can do what you want – you can generate income and you can be more flexible.'

That was the driving force behind the Belles' Project Phoenix – the desire for the club to have its own spaces both for on-pitch success and potentially its commercial impact, rather than having to share a ground with men's teams and take second or third or even fourth priority.

'I think if the FA were to enable clubs to build their own infrastructure, it would just need a big blast of input to get this all sorted,' said Lygo, 'because we're all sort of trying to keep up all the time, the ones who are not up there with the big teams – trying to scrabble together to get everything organised.'

Spring 2016

Re-Orientating

LEYTON Orient's blistering form had continued throughout the winter but the crowds were still minimal. 'We never really have fans come to our games – which is fine,' said Oly, who had moved to England from the USA to pursue her postgraduate study having played football from childhood. 'Once we decided to have a "bring a fan" day, and everyone's attitude was, "No, they won't come." I was like, "What are you talking about?" If I was in the States, everyone would come. Even if you were playing pick-up soccer, people would come and watch. It's crazy. I didn't know what to say. I couldn't tell if they were joking, but I was shocked. Your friend is playing in the FA Cup, you go and watch them play. It didn't compute for me.'

Their half-time appearance at Brisbane Road during one of the men's team's home games had been partially intended to whip up some interest among those already committed to following Orient – and coach Chris Brayford had big plans for the future.

'The players got a good reaction from the crowd – the next step is to play there,' he said. 'It went really well. The [community] trust and the club were really nice to sort that out.

'I do have that frustration that I know we're not a priority for them. From the club's perspective they used to have a partnerships manager and now it falls on the commercial director's plate. I'm going to be much more proactive in that – I don't want to be bothering them with stuff. We need to build a better relationship with the club.'

West Ham Ladies, of the Women's Premier League, had recently announced a midweek game at Upton Park against Tottenham, which was garnering a lot of publicity, and Brayford added, 'I'll speak to Orient about the possibility of a game at Brisbane Road. It might not be possible during the season, but maybe a charity game. We'll try and get that for a one-off, like West Ham.'

The players were relieved to report that they had been warmly welcomed by the club and the fans, contrary to their fears.

'It was actually really nice, it was positive!' beamed Oly. 'It seemed to be a family crowd, all different sorts, families, women, children, and it seemed like a friendly atmosphere, it wasn't aggressive.'

She stopped, and gathered her thoughts. 'The last games I went to were at QPR, where I got cursed at; some guy spent the whole game sitting next to us and saying, "That's why you don't let women into football."'

She looked slightly bewildered as she recounted the incident, and then smiled again as she returned to talk about the lovely reaction the team had got at Orient.

'Everyone had a really nice time. We had seats in the stand. Before we went, we all just met up at a pub nearby and had a drink or two, and some people brought their families and friends with them. They gave us a bunch of tickets to the game, which was nice, so we all went to the game and had nice seats!'

When they ran out, though, they were still without the Leyton Orient-branded kit they had been expecting all season. Instead, they donned Kick It Out-branded t-shirts, promoting football's anti-discrimination organisation.

'They needed to be sizes that were well-fitting – but I got a bagful of large shirts!' said Brayford. 'For some of the girls, they'd have looked like onesies or something.'

Again, he had big plans for when the kit actually arrived, perceiving it as a symbol of the men's club's commitment to the women's side.

'When we get the kit, that'll show they hold us in esteem,' he said. 'Orient fans are a brilliant bunch, and we've got to do some things to build on it.'

Their fixtures had been interrupted throughout December and January due to inclement weather and poor pitches, which is a yearly occurrence further down the football pyramid. Indeed, since their 2-0 away defeat to league leaders AFC Wimbledon in mid-December, in which Brayford maintained his side were the better of the two, Orient had had only two games, most recently a 2-1 loss to Fulham, which effectively ended their title challenge.

'Unfortunately we lost at the weekend, and one that if we hadn't had a postponement we would have won,' said Oly. 'I don't think we'll catch Wimbledon.'

She thought for a moment about the mathematical calculations that might give Orient the chance of the championship before giving up and concluding, 'I don't know what happens. Do they just make it up at the end? Every year I feel like it's been different – maybe I'm not paying attention.'

She returned to the topic of postponements. 'It's really frustrating, because you're on a roll and you're hitting mid-season form and then you just get set back and you don't really pick it up until the end of the season again. We ran into it a couple of years ago and I think last year it happened too. It's happened when we've made it further in the Capital Cup and other tournaments, when you're doing well in the season and progressing in the cup, which is important, and then you have this break, the games keep getting postponed – especially with the cup.

'I found that it really killed us, because teams that are higher up, in higher leagues, are training more regularly, they're training several times a week, and when we play those teams, it's embarrassing in the sense that what could have been possibly us winning a really tight game becomes a massive gap and then you're just dying because you haven't played in two months, and they're training three times a week.'

She cast her mind back to October and a thumping 7-2 defeat away to Tottenham, a WPL side, in the Capital Cup.

'When we played Tottenham we were watching them sprint after the game and just thinking, "Oh my God, you are so fit." When I was at college, I was that fit, because you have specific, allotted time, and it's lovely, it's great. I remember that. It was fantastic.'

Brayford was confident that there would not be too much of a backlog facing his side, intending to rearrange fixtures for midweek evenings, as an extended season would mean a change of home ground.

'We lose access to Mile End Stadium in March,' he explained, 'so we always hope to get our home games in before then. We'd play at the MatchDay centre, where Waltham Forest play. It's a commercial facility but it gets used a lot and costs us more.'

Oly and some of her team-mates got some January match practice in by entering the FA People's Cup, a five-a-side competition open to anyone who was not a professional footballer – men, women, veterans, two junior age categories plus walking football. The Leyton Orient women decided they might as well have a go.

'Lydia got an e-mail about it and wasn't sure what it was, but she was like, "Hey, anyone want to do this five-a-side? It's free!"' smiled Oly.

Lydia got seven volunteers, and signed the team up accordingly for the first round of games in Shoreditch. They were joined on the day by England legend and Arsenal coach Kelly Smith, who they spotted having her photo taken with fans and players.

'Someone was like, "That's Kelly Smith! Someone's taking a picture with her!" Then Heather was like, "I want to take a picture with Kelly Smith!"'

They did, and promptly posted it to the club social media accounts. Oly was particularly pleased to have a record of her meeting with Smith as she had followed her career for years.

'I didn't say anything to her,' she was quick to say, 'but I grew up near where she played in the States, so I knew her before I clocked that she was an England all-star. She was always in the paper, setting all the records. In high school I knew her because she was always in the college and university section of the sport. It was cool to see her.'

Of course, what happened on the pitch was more important than star-spotting, and the Orient women joined dozens of other teams in the initial group stages before being eliminated in the quarter-finals.

'You played short games, like 15 minutes, and you played everyone in your group, and then after that, it's a knockout,' explained Oly. 'We eased through our group, and it was fun – we were all joking around.'

That sense of carnival was probably why Oly was not best prepared for the day, forgetting her shin pads and her football boots.

'I borrowed someone's boots and stole-slash-borrowed someone's shin guards, someone random, who turned out to be a team who were playing in our group – they had an extra pair,' she said. 'She was so nice; she was like, "Oh yeah, you can borrow them for as long as you want, just if we get knocked out before you I'll have to take them." I was like, "You are genuinely the nicest person."'

Oly found that kindness rather refreshing after the aggression of the 11-a-side league.

'The majority of my experience specifically with women playing is in our league, some of them are super nasty, not directed necessarily at us but at each other,' she said. 'What I found nice about the FA People's Cup is how friendly it was – competitive but in the good way. Everyone that was there wanted to have a fun day out, basically, and the fun day out was playing football.'

No rain in Spain

A S the boggy English pitches stolidly made their way through the last throes of winter, Arsenal Ladies swapped their Hertfordshire base for a rather sunnier clime and began their pre-season preparation with a jaunt to Seville.

Six weeks before the start of the Women's Super League, Pedro Martinez Losa's squad spent six days on the Spain–Portugal border, training hard while finding time for drills on the beach. Those weren't necessarily the most serious exercises, though. Twitter lit up when captain Alex Scott posted a short clip of striker Natalia Pablos Sanchon, resplendent in a blindfold ready for trust-building games, running towards the sea rather than towards her partner – Scott herself, helpless with laughter at her unfortunate colleague.

Two days later, Scott was still chuckling about it. 'I've never seen her run so fast! I mean, she was running in the wrong direction,' she chortled. 'But Fara [Williams] eventually saved her, so she didn't *go* into the sea.'

It was evident the squad were enjoying their time together, revelling in the sunshine as well as the occasional game of golf.

'When you go away, you get to know people on a personal level as well,' said centre-half Jemma Rose. 'You get to know what people like, what they dislike, and that makes the team stronger.'

Rose was still relatively new in her senior career. She joined Arsenal on a full-time contract after she finished university. As a student, she had been playing semi-professionally for Bristol Academy in the WSL, but moving to London and one of the most feted women's teams in Europe was a big step.

'I was a lot more scared about moving four and a half hours away from home!' she admitted. 'Coming from Bristol, and a completely different team and style of football, to signing a full-time contract at Arsenal – it took me a long while to settle in.'

She credited Casey Stoney, her partner in central defence, for her progress as a player, which had resulted in an England call-up for that soggy game at Ashton Gate.

'Playing alongside Casey, personally I feel like I've improved a lot,' said Rose. 'Hopefully I'm going to take a lot from her; and the girls that are coming through, the younger age groups who are wanting to play in my position when they're a little bit older, I hope I can be that person they look up to, like I look up to Casey.'

'The whole tour has just been fantastic in terms of bringing a whole group of new players together,' added Scott.

Fara Williams was one of those additions. It had been rumoured for months that England's most-capped player was set to move to Meadow Park from Liverpool, and she had diplomatically avoided the question when it was asked during interviews. When she finally put pen to paper in January, it was the end of all that speculation, but also signalled what seemed to be the dawn of a new Arsenal project, drawing on top-class international talent alongside their much-vaunted youth system in order to compete with the new money of Manchester City and Chelsea.

'You would have thought Fara's been here years the way she's going on already,' grinned Scott, who admitted that she and Williams, as the senior professionals with their increased requirement for recovery time, were making good use of the Spanish siestas and enjoying their afternoon naps. 'That's her experience and her character, she can just get along with anyone. I think it's going to help a lot of the players around her, her experience, how she likes to control games. It's a massive signing for the club.'

Other elite players joined too – the Netherlands' Danielle van de Donk, Ireland's Katie McCabe, experienced enough to step right into the first-team squad, young enough to mould to the Arsenal way.

The new-look squad were faced with some top-quality opposition. First, and behind closed doors, they took on Wolfsburg, the team who knocked Arsenal out of the UEFA Women's Champions League at the semi-final stage in 2013. The German side might have notched up a 3-0 win in Spain, but the Arsenal players were by no means disappointed in their first game of 2016.

'When I've played against the Germany national team, they really work on their patterns of play, and it's exactly the same with Wolfsburg – they all know where they're going to be, it's a pinpoint cross and they score a goal,' said Scott. 'The Wolfsburg players will tell you the scoreline didn't reflect the game.'

'The three goals were all from crosses – I think it was a lack of concentration from us,' suggested Rose.

The squad had three full days to regroup after that match and prepare for their second and final match of the tour, against Bayern Munich at the Estadio Olimpico as part of the city's women's football festival. It was a rather strangely organised event, with an alarm screeching from the stadium over the city as fans queued for entry, and the public announcement system struggling to make itself heard. In the warm-up match, Real Betis's under-18 girls against their local rivals Seville, the assistant referees were not equipped with flags, and spent the first half waving training vests instead.

Regardless of the chaos, scores of junior squads filled the stands, excited to see their heroines, many of whom they had seen only on television previously. They were particularly thrilled to welcome their compatriots – Bayern's Veronica Boquete, plus Arsenal's Spanish trio, Marta Corredera, Vicky Losada and Natalia. All four were treated as superstars. They posed for photos, signed autographs, gave out merchandise, and waved every time their names were sung – Losada smiled throughout even as her warm-ups from the bench were interrupted as her fans clamoured for her attention.

'Are any of the girls from Seville?' was the obvious question. 'No,' replied Arsenal's press officer, who had clearly been asked it before. 'They're just really famous here.'

The crowd were also treated to a truly marvellous display of football from both sides, with Arsenal running out deserved 3-1 winners. It was, obviously, appropriate that Natalia came off the bench to add a classy brace of goals, but that came after Jordan Nobbs had opened the scoring with a magnificent long-range strike.

'I had a feeling as soon as I let it go that it was going in, so it was a great feeling to score,' said Nobbs afterwards.

She had spent months struggling with injury, with her World Cup restricted due to a hamstring niggle that just would not go away. Arsenal noticed her absence more keenly, missing her creativity, tenaciousness and occasional spark of genius. A fully-fit Nobbs alongside Fara Williams would have brought joy to any Arsenal fan. Both of them have been known for their penchant for spectacular free kicks, but Nobbs guaranteed no infighting over the set pieces.

'We'll just know when we want it. As long as I'm playing well and Fara is as well, it's a plus for our side that we have more opportunities and more people to take long-range chances,' she said, before adding with a twinkle, 'If I'm scoring in normal play, then I don't mind Fara having a few free kicks!'

The quality of Arsenal's performance so early in their pre-season was perhaps slightly surprising, but it was also good to see for anyone who wishes for a more competitive WSL. The Arsenal players were already confident after just two games that they would be genuine title contenders in 2016.

'The way we played out there was phenomenal,' enthused Nobbs. 'We looked organised, we looked ready, we looked fit. We did a lot of stuff as a team. I think it's showing what Pedro's trying to develop this year. It's slowly ticking over now that he's settled in a little bit – and it showed today on the pitch.'

'At Arsenal we've got very high expectations. We always want to win things, historically Arsenal always have won things, and we're never going to stop wanting to win things,' said Rose. 'The fight and determination is always going to be there.'

In the second tier

OVER the past few years, London Bees have found themselves overshadowed by the other WSL teams based in the capital.

Head coach Julian Broomes left the club shortly after the end of the 2015 season, having been in post for just over a year. His team's performances had been less than spectacular, ending the campaign with two 8-0 defeats in August, two single-goal losses in September, and a 7-1 thrashing in the final home game of the season. A 4-0 win against Watford in September and a last-match goalless away draw against the same opposition could not hide the fact that this was a struggling team failing to respond to instructions, and finding itself massively outclassed by the opposition. They finished the season third from bottom, with a goal difference of -34.

The players began to drift away from The Hive at the start of January, many of them heading south of the river to Millwall Lionesses. Rebecca Sawiuk had just been appointed as head coach at The Den, and she knew the Bees players well from her time in charge there prior to Broomes's appointment.

When David Edmondson – the former coach of Bristol Academy – was unveiled as the new man in charge of Bees at the end of January, he had a much depleted squad waiting to greet him.

'No first-team player has signed at the moment,' he said at the start of February. 'It's really busy trying to find players and get something to start working with. It probably wasn't the best environment here at times last year from what I understand, and from talking to a couple of the players who are still here training at the moment.

'My appointment is really quite recent, so a few players were tempted away through a timescale or through a little bit of disillusionment from the last year or two and just needed a new challenge. For me, it's not really, it's pointless worrying about people who've gone, you've just got to concentrate on who's here now and who can we get in, and work with those players. I'm a big advocate of looking forward rather than looking back. If players have gone, that's their choice – I'm worried about the ones who are here and the ones who will be here.'

Before he formally took on the role, his side had an FA Cup game against fellow WSL2 side Durham, who had finished just one place above them in the league in the previous season. The inexperienced Bees side, mostly from the development squad, quickly found themselves shipping goals, and Edmondson stepped into the changing room at half-time to motivate the disheartened team.

'While I wasn't taking the team I came in at half-time and had a chat with them, and said, "Look, we take the second half five minutes at a time," and they did really well. In the last eight or nine minutes I think three goals went in, but the previous half an hour in the second half was very positive.'

After a poor 2015 and less than ideal preparations for the new season, Edmondson had been talking to his players to encourage them to approach the new campaign as professionally as possible.

'We had a meeting and I did a little bit of a review with them and got their input – an assessment of things we needed to stop, things that we needed to keep doing, and things that we needed to start doing,' he explained. 'It was very much a case of it coming from the players, saying, "One of the major things we've got to stop is the negativity, we've got to stop the capitulation when they do go behind or concede a goal."

'That was coming from them, that wasn't coming from me: that was their comments. All I can say is all I've seen since I've been here is really positive girls working hard, girls being positive on the pitch. I'm not here to comment on what's gone on before, I can only deal with what's here now and what I'm going to be responsible for, as long as we can stay positive and realise that we're in it together. We probably won't win every game this year, there will be disappointments and we just have to deal with them and be prepared to do that.'

Although WSL2 sides are considered semi-professional, there are degrees of that. Some of the stronger sides are heading towards full-time professionalism, while others continue to pick up their expenses, with contracts guaranteeing only the national minimum wage for the hours worked. Edmondson took over a Bees side with work and education commitments, but emphasised that being semi-professional should not affect their attitude towards football. His squad were scheduled to train on two evenings a week, a schedule he was still considering.

'We try and timetable the training so that it works around [their employment and study],' he explained. 'We're understanding of the fact that girls do have other things in their lives, whether that's work or whether that's study or whatever it is, but basically we ask that when we are training, it's creating that balance and making sure that when we're here, it's making sure that we get the most out of it. We've got two hours when we're actually on the grass but there's time around that when there's psychological work to be done, there's preparation work to be done in the gym, and then we get out on the grass, so it's maximising the time that you are together. I don't want girls here for two or three hours and an hour of that is wasted because we're sat around, having a chat, not getting out on the pitch. Let's maximise every minute that we're here.

'It's about behaviours, so it's getting into the ethos of, "Yes, we're here to train, and it is work – while we're here, we're working." It's not just a social gathering where we get to have a chat and see what we've done the rest of the week; it is literally from when we walk into the gym we are working, both physically and mentally, and we are getting prepared. It is a balancing act. So far the girls have been fantastic: attitude has been great, training has been high intensity, they seem to be enjoying it, lots of positive comments.

'As we're getting closer to the season, we'll get a bit more tied down into who is actually going to be playing and get into the specifics of how we're going to play. At the moment it's really about how we're getting to a base level and doing some football conditioning, and just getting the basics around how I want us to play.'

Any team hoping to be in the top half of WSL2 at the end of 2016 would have been extremely excited about the season to come, with two promotion slots on offer. Edmondson was rather more cautious and guarded about the months ahead.

'We had this discussion on my first night,' he admitted, adding, 'I think realistically it's consolidation [as a target for London Bees], especially when you look around. There's two or three teams in WSL2 who are basically full-time and there's a couple of huge loan deals that have been done from top WSL1 teams. There's probably three or four teams pushing for those top two promotion spots – but I also said I've never entered a game of football not trying to win it. While if you're being super-sensible and getting a realistic head on, it's consolidation this season for Bees, that does mean an improvement.

'We have to be improving from week to week and from season to season. We will enter every game trying to win it.

If we get some good results early you never know what can happen. I'm not writing anything off. Our aim is always to be better than last week, and to keep doing that. We need to see what that does in terms of results; it's really difficult in the off-season to say. If anyone looks at us at the moment, they wouldn't expect a great deal – but that will change dramatically in the next couple of weeks, and I'm sure it will with some other clubs as well.'

※ ※ ※ ※ ※

David Parker was also regrouping his squad up at Birmingham, still reeling from the departure of Karen Carney. He was philosophical about the loss.

'The players we've had that have come and gone – we've put them on the stage,' he said. 'Look at Jodie Taylor, no one knew her before she came to Birmingham, she'd been playing abroad – we helped her rejuvenate her career before she moved on to Sweden. Rachel Williams was the big hitter for the first couple of seasons, then obviously moved on to Chelsea. Laura Bassett as well, Eni Aluko – that's a third of the World Cup squad who have played at Birmingham, or come through the ranks as a development player, so it's nothing new.

'We've always been that club who have produced the best players in the country and sent them on to bigger and better things. That's just our place in the world. Fortunately for the club and the fans we've massively overachieved for four years. That's the reality. We haven't had star names or even signed star names, we've helped make them become star names, and that's always been our ethos and our way forward – nothing will change from that. Players will come and go, move on to bigger and better things, if that's over in America, or in Germany, Sweden, which we've done before, then so be it.'

Since the changes in the WSL system removing the strict wage cap that had existed at the league's inception, smaller clubs with less money coming in from their allied men's team were finding it more challenging to compete, and Parker was accepting of that too as he prepared for the 2016 campaign and beyond.

'We will always be behind in the money stakes because of the stature of the men's club against the big Premier League teams – that's never ever going to change,' he said without a trace of bitterness. 'What we do have to look at is how we do things. We built a squad we had for a couple of years; we were close to winning the league, we should have won the league, really, and always fell short. Then we built a new team and got to the Champions League semi-final based on youth players, and players who'd given us a bit of the core over the previous two seasons. It's nothing unusual to overachieve.

'I'm not expecting the same, we need to stabilise a bit this year in the coming months until we transition properly as a football club and get ourselves a better infrastructure. That will take a bit of time, but after that, I've got really great hopes. Everything that the men's club have spoken to us about, everything that we've looked to do and build upon – I think we just need to stabilise a little bit for the moment, and then we can be a massive force again.'

A fan of the summer scheduling, he had had the chance to examine the fixture list and the structure of the cup competitions, and had some of his own ideas about how that could be improved in the future.

'I think realistically we do need more games on a domestic front within a league campaign,' he said. 'Maybe eight teams with three games each, 21 games. I think it's too much too fast with ten teams. I think the FA's tried to do it in the right way but has expanded too quick too soon. They went for a Super League 2 and then added on top of that a development [youth] squad as well. You can see from the quality when you go out and watch the development squads, we've been playing a bunch of 16- and 17-year-olds and they're top of the league. That shouldn't be happening. Our youngsters are good, don't get me wrong, but they should be mid-table, not walking away with the league in the development squad, the under-21 league, so the players' quality and depth is really scratchy. You need to be careful how you keep progressing it because otherwise you deteriorate the quality by stretching the resources too thin, which isn't going to help them.'

He was also disappointed at the removal of the round-robin stage of the Continental Cup for 2016.

'I think the group stage was crucial, I think it was brilliant. Look at what Arsenal and Chelsea did – they played all the kids, so they got first-team opportunities, they were playing games. That's not going to be the case now – there's not a manager in the country who's going to risk getting knocked out of the cup in the knockout rounds,' he said. 'They'll be lucky if they get two games a season, so it's going to be hard for managers to see how the playing field develops.'

※ ※ ※ ※ ※

Jodie Michalska crushed all in her path during the 2014/15 season. Then 28 years old, she fired Sheffield to the promotion play-offs with 30 goals, finishing as the WPL Northern Division's top scorer and the players' player of the year – both for the second season running.

She may not have scored the winner in the championship play-off against Portsmouth but she was quite content with that. The long-serving Lisa Giampalma got the only goal of the game in stoppage time and it was as important to Michalska as if she had netted it herself.

'Lisa scoring that goal meant more to me than me scoring a hat-trick because of all she's been through with the club,' she said. 'She's been there for eight, nine years, at the bottom of the women's pyramid, and worked her way up, so it meant a lot. I care about all the girls. Even though I got top goalscorer, and I've won it more or less every time I've played in that league, it's a team effort. I was really proud of her for that one. It was very emotional.'

Michalska started her career as a central midfielder, signing for Sheffield United at the age of 16, moving up front when the coaches there spotted her pace.

'I got a hat-trick in my first game and that was it, I was a centre-forward,' she said. 'I'd never really had any proper coaching on how to be a centre-forward, but watching football I used to like Thierry Henry. I loved his style, loved the way he played, so in my earlier years that's who I'd look to in terms of technique, but other than that I've just become my own person.'

She has only played for three clubs during her career – Sheffield United, Lincoln Ladies and now Sheffield – and has always loved the family feeling at her current club. That loyalty to her team-mates has been her inspiration to play, and that was rewarded with their triumph and step up to WSL2.

'Teams would turn up and they'd have five members of staff, and we'd turn up with Mitch [Helen Mitchell] and they'd be like, "We're going to hammer you,"' she laughed. 'It just felt good that we did it for her, and all the effort she put in, because she goes unrecognised and has gone unrecognised for so many years now. It meant a lot that Mitch got the recognition last season with the awards that she won [including WPL manager of the year]. I'm happy about that.'

After the promotion, though, Michalska felt somewhat unsettled. Mitchell's move into the role of general manager and the arrival of Mick Mulhern to take over responsibility for the team did not help with that.

'Last season everybody played for each other, we played for Mitch, we played for the club. It's a totally different feeling now,' she said, admitting that she did not as a rule embrace change. 'It is the end of an era. I'm struggling coping with it, if I'm honest. If we change the warm-up on a Sunday, it messes with my head, I don't like it. "Why are we doing a different warm-up?" I can't adjust.'

Michalska was having difficulty adapting to having a new manager after Mitchell had shaped the entire Sheffield set-up.

'Mitch is such a great people person,' she said. 'She genuinely cares about every single player: whether it's first-team, development, she genuinely cares. You felt that. I can't describe the feeling that you got. You came to training and whether it was a good session or a bad session it just felt good. Now it's different, because there's a new guy that's come in, and new players, it's just not the same, there's no emotion there any more. I play off emotion.'

Indeed, Michalska was even considering retirement at the end of the promotion season.

'I quit, chucked my boots and everything away,' she declared. Her intent was to have a baby – who would be her second – but her plans changed.

'It was like, "Oh, it's not happened yet, can I come and play for the development side?"' she said ruefully. 'I came to play but I wasn't really getting fit or that involved, because I thought it was only temporary. Then the first team came back, and I thought I'd train with the first team until I know what's happening.'

After a discussion with her partner over Christmas 2015, they agreed that Michalska would play for one more season.

'I'm not bothered, it means nothing to me,' she admitted. 'It wouldn't make any difference in the Northern Prem, in the Combination or in the WSL; as long as the team around me were good, I don't care where we're playing.'

The lure of WSL2 was not particularly strong for Michalska. She had the chance to play in the early stages of the WSL when she was with Lincoln Ladies (the club which has since become Notts County), but put her football career on hold to undergo IVF treatment to have her daughter.

'The manager had kept saying, "Don't do it, leave it another year, because we're going to get this bid, play WSL with me," and I said, "I can't, I can't put my life on hold,"' she recalled. 'My family is my life, not football. I'm committed when I'm playing, but ultimately my family is my life. I found out I was pregnant the day before it got announced they'd got the Super League, so I missed out with Lincoln. Later, he came to my house to offer me a contract and I went training, but it just wasn't for me – it was too far when I'd got a little one.'

Even though one might expect a player to be overjoyed to have the chance to step up into the competition's elite, Michalska maintained that she was more interested in playing for a team of a decent standard and with a good atmosphere. Still, her partner was keen for her to test herself at a higher level, and she felt she had another season in her at least.

So Michalska bought herself a new pair of boots and attempted to get in the right frame of mind for competing in WSL2. She wondered whether she needed to relax a little more to help her cope with the changes at Sheffield; she had a full-time job as general manager of a vending machine firm as well as devoting time to her five-year-old daughter at home.

'We're a social enterprise. The lads I've got in the warehouse have come on a talent match scheme; they might have struggled gaining employment before, or struggled in their early life, we've given them a chance.

'It can be challenging, very challenging at times,' she said, 'but I used to gain my enjoyment away from that with football. I'd be like, "Forget about work, I'm coming to football!" and just enjoy it.'

Even though Sheffield's players had to cope with a lengthy gap at the end of their promotion season, Michalska's changing plans did at least mean her fitness levels were high.

'It's been easier for me because I was retiring so I prepared for that, and then I played a little bit with the development, so I got a little bit of fitness in that,' she said. 'It hasn't been quite as long for me, but for some of the girls when they came in for their first sessions, they were struggling because it had been such a long time. No matter how much you're running it's not the same as playing football.'

Although Michalska's love for playing had remained constant, she was not a fan of watching women's football, preferring the men's game. That meant she had little knowledge of the defences that would be waiting for her in WSL2.

'I wouldn't know who any of the defenders are!' she said. 'I got to know them in the Northern Prem because I played against them for so many years, but I couldn't even name a centre-half in the WSL.'

She was, however, happy that there was a second division of the WSL, that Sheffield would be competing in it – and that her team-mates and friends were getting publicity and public recognition for their achievements.

'It's good that we're finally getting recognised,' she said. 'We're going about our business a little bit different.'

Building for the future

PROJECT Phoenix was progressing apace in the spring of 2016 and Doncaster Belles chairwoman Faye Lygo was evidently happy with their achievements to that point.

'We've now completed the house that was being refurbished, so the players have now moved in,' she said. 'We've started planning work on the ground – we're just working out where the pitches will lie exactly, the seeding season is just about to start. I have commenced planning applications for one of the outbuildings to be converted into a strength and conditioning facility.

'We had to have a bird survey and they found evidence of owls feeding, so it's just delayed things slightly; while it won't prevent planning, it just means depending on what they're doing it might mean we have to do certain things with the roofs.'

The club were spacing out their building plans over the next few months, partly in order to attract external funding, and Lygo was quick to add, just in case, 'It doesn't sound much when you quickly say it!'

Of course, that was plenty – and there was much more going on as well, including the club's application to become a regional talent centre, and planning for the forthcoming season in WSL1.

'We've had reasonable changeover of players,' she said. 'There's a particular player I haven't signed who couldn't commit to the increased sessions due to childcare arrangements. It wasn't that we got rid of a whole sweep of players: for some of them, it just didn't suit what they were wanting, they might not be first choice, they might just be sitting on the bench. A couple of them have gone to lower-level clubs where they should be and deserve to be first choice straight on, so we've had some goodbyes.'

Not all of the Belles were switching to full-time professional contracts, but some were, and Lygo was happy with that as a starting point, particularly with the influx of established pros to the squad.

'We wanted to follow the Sunderland method of not abandoning all our team and not starting anew, but we knew we needed to make some key signings, some marquee signings, and make a statement, because we don't want to be struggling, we want to be a solid member of WSL1, and then work from there,' she said. 'As Leicester [then top of the Premier League] are showing in the men's, you don't have to have a big income to be doing quite well. We knew that there were areas [we needed to improve] – fitness was the biggest area, and you could see that in our games against Liverpool and Man City [in the 2015 Continental Cup] where we held our own but in the second half we weakened, but that's the difference between being part-time and full-time, I think.'

The players were thrilled at the progress of the club. Courtney Sweetman-Kirk had grabbed the headlines in 2015, as WSL2's top scorer and players' player of the year, and she was relishing the chance of professionalisation that Doncaster Belles were now offering her and the rest of the squad. She was particularly pleased that professional football was becoming a potential career choice for young girls in the local area, starting with the younger members of the squad who were playing around their school and university study.

'It's something looking forward to the next ten years, something that can hopefully make a massive impact in that area of the country and something that girls can look forward to,' she said. 'It's something I didn't have at that age, thinking being a full-time footballer is a viable career path, but now girls are growing up knowing that's what they can do, and having Project Phoenix in the area, it's there on the doorstep, and it's something to aim towards.'

Sweetman-Kirk joined Belles in 2014, from Notts County, having played for their previous incarnation Lincoln Ladies. The 25-year-old scored 25 goals in 2015, and after such a successful season, she was looking forward to the challenges of 2016.

'I scored a lot of goals and that made me feel good on a personal note,' she said. 'Getting that formal recognition – in terms of the players' player as well, that's the award that every player wants to win, to be recognised by your peers, it's not just one club, it's all the clubs. To know that I've conducted myself in the right way and people see the work that I'm trying to put in, and how hard I work, that's massive. I picked up a couple of awards at the Donny awards as well, so I think it's been a very pleasing season for me, but hopefully it's something to build on and try and surpass that next season.'

She was preparing to partner England's Natasha Dowie in the Belles' attack, and was relishing the chance to link up with and learn from such an experienced player.

'I'm viewing it as a massive opportunity!' she enthused. 'I'm massively excited to work with Tash; we're quite different in terms of the way we play so I think more than anything we'll complement each other and hopefully we can scare a lot of defences and score a lot of goals together.

'It's a great time to be involved with the club, the big signings we're getting, I think it shows the ambition of the club and where it's going, and personally for me it's exciting times getting a full-time contract and getting to train day in, day out with the likes of Natasha Dowie and Becky Easton and Katrin [Omarsdottir], it's a great opportunity and it's something that we're all very much looking forward to.'

Sweetman-Kirk was not setting any goalscoring targets for 2016 but she was confident that she and the team would prove more than ready for the rigours of WSL1.

'I'm sure if we put the work in we can compete with anyone,' she said. 'We did it last season at home against Sunderland: we beat them, and they were WSL1. Talking of Sunderland, if you look at what they did last season, you can go up from WSL2 to 1 and definitely compete, and that's something that we will take a lot of confidence from. I think it's just about being confident in yourself and what you've got and hopefully showing that on the pitch.

'We're raring to go and ready to get into it. Me personally, I've got itchy feet, I want to get playing. Playing WSL football you get used to the mid-season break, you have to learn how to keep momentum going and keep yourself geed up, but at the same time getting the rest that you need. It was nice to have a rest over Christmas and spend time with family, but now it's all about getting ready for next season.'

Sweetman-Kirk was already eyeing up the WSL1 centre-halves and looking forward to testing herself against them.

'Last season we played Man City in the Conti Cup and it was nice to play against Steph [Houghton], the England captain, it's always nice to gauge where you're at, but there's fantastic players all the way across WSL1, so anyone I can try and terrorise I'll play against!' she laughed. 'We'll see when we get there.'

Lygo was pleased that the players were so happy. 'People might think it's cheesy, but there is this real feeling of Belles family,' she said. 'People have commented on it at the club – it is actually a real thing. I put it down to the fact that we've got

Sheila Edmunds, who is a founder member, Julie Chipchase, who played for us, managed us, and is now one of the most qualified women coaches in the country – I think all of that ties us all together, that meaning, they care so passionately about the club, and that comes across. Everyone wants to make everyone else happy, and it is that kind of family feel.'

※ ※ ※ ※ ※

It was a chilly day in Hertfordshire, and the press conference lounge in London Colney was packed out with journalists desperately filing their copy. Arsene Wenger, manager of the Arsenal men's team, had just given his thoughts to the world on how he thought his team would do in their crunch fixture against Manchester United at the weekend. A win would improve their title credentials, under pressure from their north London rivals Tottenham Hotspur and the moneybags of Manchester City.

At the back of the room, hovering around the coffee machine, were a small group of journalists less interested in Monsieur Wenger than they were in Senor Pedro Martinez Losa. Arsenal Ladies were hosting a media day immediately after the press conference, giving interested media representatives the chance to tour the new facilities available to the women's team and take a look at one of their training sessions.

The plan was evidently to scoop up some of the writers lingering after Wenger's press conference and offer them another potential story from the women's game, but deadlines are pressing and old habits are hard to break. It was primarily the usual suspects there to see the benefits Arsenal's investment in women's football has reaped. There were also some TV crews, always alert to potentially useable footage, putting together packages on the always media-friendly Alex Scott, who completed her degree in sports journalism while preparing for England duty at the Women's World Cup, and had just announced that she was going to be a contestant on Bear Grylls's next TV series, filmed a few months previously in top-secret conditions.

'It was one of the toughest experiences of my life, but that's what I wanted,' she said. 'I wanted to be taken out of my comfort zone – who is Alex Scott as a person, away from football? I've been at Arsenal since I was eight, so it gave me the opportunity to experience something different and at the same time still try and represent women's football in a positive light. Obviously coming off the back of the World Cup, to be given an opportunity to do a show like that, it was a bigger picture. It wasn't just about, "Yeah, I want to go and do it," it was more, "How can I make this work for women's football, for Arsenal, and myself and my future career?"'

Scott already had plans for her future career, submitting the final pieces of coursework for her degree while she was in Canada in the summer of 2015.

'I never wanted to get to the end of my career and think, "What's next?" so it's fortunate that I've been able to combine the two,' she explained. 'For me, I'm not the sort of person who panics or stresses myself, I use my time effectively, I don't go home and switch off and leave things until the last minute, so it was hard juggling the degree with training commitments and preparing for a World Cup, but it's manageable if you manage yourself in the right way.'

That wasn't to say that she was already planning for life after football. Aged 31, she was simply weighing up her options and working to avoid a career chasm when she did decide to hang up her boots.

'I've never put a date on when I want to end,' she said. 'For me, the moment it's a chore to come into training, it's a chore to turn up and train hard, that's when I'll know that I need to stop, but at the moment I feel great, I'm still enjoying being here, in this new environment.'

She was referring to the new training facilities specifically for Arsenal Ladies – sparkling and modern. They may not be elaborate – or at least not yet – but this is a functional hub devoted just to female footballers. For Scott, formerly so critical of what the club provided for its women's side, this is a major step forward.

'Having our new training base, our new structure, I think it does make you feel a lot more like a professional,' she said. 'Over the years, when we talked about the women's game going professional, everyone just jumped on it thinking money-wise. Well, no, to be an ultimate professional is about the training facilities and how you train, and this gives us the opportunity to do that, which is great.'

Faye White, former Arsenal and England captain and now in charge of marketing for the women, was the tour guide, showing the journalists round the offices, past the physio's surgery, and into the changing rooms. The squad's shirts were all hanging neatly on their pegs, each appropriately name-labelled, with a few spare nearest the door. The plan was, White explained, for new players, whether from outside or promoted from the youth squad, to take those spots. Then as other players retired or moved on, everyone would move round; the pegs nearest the door would always be for those lowest in the long-serving stakes.

'You've got to earn your stripes!' cackled an eavesdropping Scott.

Next door to the changing room is a lounge area, with gigantic squashy sofas and a big-screen TV. Next to the television, though, is an equally large wipe-clean tactics board, and in the middle of the floor is a conference table should any discussions be required.

On this day with the media, players were taking turns holding forth in a group interview.

Jordan Nobbs was happy to talk about the club's invest-ment in the women's facilities. She had just signed an extension to her contract and was looking forward to her future with Arsenal.

'It's crazy to see the facilities now that we have,' she said. 'I think it's exciting for Arsenal as a club to have. If we have the players like Fara Williams and exciting new players from abroad, I think it's only a positive for us as a team. That's why I'm wanting to commit more of my future here. I've loved it since the age of 17 and we've only taken more steps forward.

'As a player you always have to look to see if the whole club is improving. A major part of me signing was for the love of the club and how I've progressed as a player. I think you have to think of yourself as an individual first and then see all the things around that. I do believe in why I signed here: we are looking to win the league, to get into the Champions League and compete against the best teams.'

Eventually the players were called away; they are expected in every morning and begin their training session just after noon. The training ground is high-security, shared as it is by the men's squads, and the security staff were keen to ensure that everyone understood that the same rules apply to media reporting on the women as well.

The group of journalists were escorted to a roped-off area by the side of the training pitch furthest away from the buildings, and the Ladies were running through their warm-ups on the side of the pitch furthest away from the media. A quiet word from the ever-watchful Faye White in the ears of Martinez Losa and his coaching team brought the squad closer.

Observing any team's training session is instructive. During the 2015 season, injured player-coach Kelly Smith was often a dominant figure in the pre-match warm-ups, with Martinez Losa taking a step back. Today, Martinez Losa was very clearly the man in charge; a newly-fit Smith was part of the squad.

'Good, Fara!' he called to his new signing, and throughout the drills he was shouting similarly encouraging words of praise to each of the squad; each of them was being watched and their work appreciated, from senior players to the youngsters to the new signings – Josephine Henning, the Germany international, had recently put pen to paper and was obviously still settling in at this point, looking quiet but intensely dedicated to her exercises. Martinez Losa was emphasising the importance of quality of movement and passing – ideas that have long-dominated the Arsenal Ladies' philosophy of football; what the veteran winger Rachel Yankey has previously described, with a certain amount of justified satisfaction, as 'the Arsenal way'.

Of course, the Arsenal way over the years has also been a successful way, as well as an aesthetically pleasing approach to playing football. Since a team of women playing in Aylesbury were lured under the Arsenal banner some decades ago, under the eye of the men's long-serving kit man Vic Akers, the team have been consistently challenging for trophies. In 2016, in the new professional era of women's football, it had taken them some time to catch up, but their facilities alongside the men went some way to proving that Arsenal were finally taking their women seriously – and putting their money where their mouth was.

England believes

AS the WPL and WSL2 sides battled it out in the fourth round of the FA Cup, the Lionesses were back on a plane – this time flying to the USA for the SheBelieves tournament. They would be taking on the hosts, France and Germany – a stern test for a team hoping to prove their superiority in Europe in 2017.

In the run-up to the tournament, coach Mark Sampson had been quoted as saying, 'The SheBelieves Cup will be a massive challenge for us – we are competing against the top three teams in the world, so it doesn't get much tougher.

'We have selected a group of players who we feel have the qualities we want the Lionesses to demonstrate when representing our group.

'With an intense schedule our focus will be on being a strong group, working hard and concentrating 100 per cent on one game at a time.

'I am confident with the players we have selected we can go to the US and be competitive in the tournament.'

The players themselves were thrilled to be competing on such an impressive stage against tough opposition.

'It's such a busy time – it's a weird time to have internationals when you're preparing for a season, but you can't turn down the competition that it is, playing against the USA, France and Germany,' said Arsenal captain Alex

Scott. 'They're the games that really test you. It's easy to do it, no disrespect, in the qualifying games against Montenegro and stuff, people can get carried away with themselves and thinking they're ready to play at the top level, but these are the real challenges that players need to step up and show that they can be an international footballer.'

Her club team-mate Jordan Nobbs was equally excited. 'I think it's the only way England can carry on that winning mentality, to play the best,' she said. 'I think we need to be playing under pressure, in big games with big crowds, to then go to world stages and European championships and compete under pressure in that role as well. It's easy playing at home against some of the lesser teams, but I think now the mentality and the drive is to be competing with the bigger and better [teams].'

Nobbs had had a disappointing 2015, with her World Cup interrupted by a hamstring injury that refused to clear up. She always enjoyed England duty, appointed to her position as the team's vice-captain at the tender age of 22.

'It was a crazy moment for me to achieve something like that,' she admitted. 'I'm very honoured to be not just part of the team but vice-captain. I love that role, it's also helped me with my role at Arsenal: to be a leader, and learn from Mark [Sampson, the team coach] and Steph [Houghton, the captain] at England, to improve me as that type of player.'

It wasn't an entirely new experience for her, taking on that kind of responsibility.

'As a kid I was always captain at England youth level, through the age groups,' she said. 'To now be alongside great players at Arsenal, great players at England, I really think I can carry on that leadership role – and hopefully one day I'll be part of that at Arsenal. Right now I'm still young and still progressing and vice-captain for England is still that next stepping stone for me to show what I can do on and off the pitch.'

She confessed that one day she would love to be England captain in her own right, but was quick to note that it was still early in her career and she was happy as second-in-command to Houghton.

'Naturally I'm learning a lot off Steph, I think she does a fantastic job, and any opportunity I get to wear the armband is an honour,' she said. 'Even just at my age being the vice-captain I feel privileged to take on that role – and I think Steph fully deserves the role she has as well.'

Excitingly for the UK-based viewer, all the England matches were aired live on the BBC. England's warm-up before the 2015 Women's World Cup had been screened on the red button, as had all their home qualifiers for Euro 2017, but away matches have historically proved a problem – mostly because they rely on a host broadcaster overseas making the rights available.

England's first match of the tournament was against the hosts in the Raymond James Stadium in Tampa, Florida; both Mark Sampson and USA coach Jill Ellis had made changes to their World Cup line-ups. Seventeen-year-old Mallory Pugh featured for the USA alongside Carli Lloyd, the woman who scored a hat-trick in the 2015 World Cup Final; Chelsea's Gilly Flaherty joined Steph Houghton in the centre of the England defence instead of Laura Bassett, with Demi Stokes playing on the wing. No defence or goalkeeper could have done anything about the single goal of the game, a piece of spectacular skill from USA substitute Crystal Dunn.

'I think we have high expectations of the [England] team nowadays, and I know they do too,' said former England captain Faye White. 'They're world champions, they have a lot of changes in their team, they had a lot of retirements after the World Cup – but there's still something about America. It's a friendly and it's good preparation, that's the most important thing; we're not a team that just defends against the likes of Germany and America any more, and we look to go for the win as well. There weren't a lot of chances in the game, but it took a pretty spectacular strike to beat us, so that's encouraging.'

England lost 3-2 to Germany before managing a goalless draw against France; but instead of the evident challenges facing the team on the pitch, some attention was rightly focused on Fara Williams, picking up her 150th cap – a landmark achievement.

Forever
blowing bubbles

THE Olympic Stadium might be where the men's club had firmly fixed its eyes over recent years, but the Boleyn Ground still held a certain amount of magic. A West Ham team playing there benefited from the special atmosphere, under the watchful twin gazes of club legends Trevor Brooking and Bobby Moore.

For West Ham Ladies to play there was even more momentous. On a freezing March evening in miserable drizzle they made their debut at the famous old ground, playing a WPL fixture against London rivals Tottenham Hotspur. More than that, they attracted 1,741 people there to watch them.

Many were obviously family and friends of the players – that much was evident from the localised cheering when names were announced by YouTube star Spencer Owen. Many, though, were fans of the men's teams, attracted by the club names, and resplendent in colours, unafraid to cheer on their representatives. They may not have noticed but the most striking thing about the crowd was the lack of segregation, allowing West Ham fans and Tottenham fans to mingle, sit alongside each other, chat, leap to their feet and express their emotions. Perhaps that should be how all football is, but a game between the two men's teams would never countenance such integration for fear of violence. It was a refreshing sight.

The game – if sometimes lacking in quality in the final third – was a tight one, and perhaps it was inevitable that it should be settled with a dubious penalty, converted well by proud captain Katie Bottom. The atmosphere, if generally supportive, as one might expect from an essentially amateur fixture, occasionally blazed into life, drawing upon the storied local enmity – Spurs defender Alex Keown bore the brunt of it, booed relentlessly for a nasty incident where her studs appeared to catch the face of the prone Whitney Locke; and there was even a brief moment when a couple of players squared up to each other. This was not the gentle, Corinthian-spirited sport executed for fun by sporting amateurs that some may have expected from the women's game.

'It happened at short notice,' said West Ham Ladies' co-chairman Stephen Hunt. 'We finally agreed a date in early February for [a game in] March, so it was crazy, we didn't have time to think about it. I'm sure if we'd started planning it in August we could have done more, but it would have been even more work.'

He was pleased to see his players so happy to be on the Boleyn turf – but also delighted that it meant just as much to their opponents. Indeed, Tottenham were already talking about hosting a reciprocal event at White Hart Lane.

'At this sort of level, any major stadium game is good for any player,' he said. 'On some level it's fulfilling a fantasy, every fan would like to do the same.'

He acknowledged that many men's clubs were still not quite sure how to negotiate their relationship with an affiliated women's team.

'Everyone's exploring what to do with it – nobody knows whether or not it's going to fully take off or not. I think the major clubs are seeing a huge growth in participation in women's football, and they're aware, and they're interested, but they don't quite understand it, and so they're torn between seeing it as an amateur kicking-around and something that's really going to fly.

'I think on one level they don't like the idea of a team in their colours not playing as well as the men, as it were, and then at the same time they're drawn by the concept of this could be another use for the stadium: every other week, men, women, men, women, at the ultimate level. They don't know which way to jump. The economics drives everything. The more fans you get, the more everyone else crowds round it.'

Hunt had spent much of his time as co-chairman building up a relationship with the men's club, and was honest about the challenges that task had presented.

'I've gone in to bat for the ladies,' he explained. 'Given that they're a £100m–£200m turnover business with an international brand, and we're an amateur club, there's a massive conceptual difference in the two. We don't talk the same language. So what I've spent most of my time doing is trying to create a structure, a means of communication that the main club can understand. Once they understand us, I think a lot of the issues disappear.

'Essentially we are hoofing around with their brand and every time we say something bad on Twitter it can all kick off. It's a case of us learning their system, complying with their system, and appreciating that we are handling a very valuable brand that people pay a lot of money for. We have a certain amount of responsibility, so if we meet them halfway and create structures, create reporting systems, behave in a way they can understand, then I think that helps.

'We are a completely independent legal structure, but working together. I think there's no incentive for them to treat us badly, but it doesn't make any sense from their point of view to put lots of money into it. It makes no commercial sense, which I appreciate.'

Hunt already had a background in business when he took on the role of chair of West Ham Ladies, describing himself as 'a fairly tough negotiator'. He saw an advertisement for the position of chairman, and it immediately set him thinking.

'My dad's always said, "Oh, my son, when he's rich, he'll buy me West Ham and make me chairman." I rang him up and said, "How would you like to be chairman of West Ham United LFC?" And he said, "Sorry, what's the small print?" We teased it for a bit, and I said, "Why don't I apply?" So I sent a very jokey application in, pointing out that I'd previously bought my dad "chairman for the day" at the West Ham players' awards in the auction, and we'd beaten Swansea, so we had a 100 per cent record of chairmanship. But I've got a strong business background in turnaround of defunct companies, and it struck me – who better than us, really? As a gift to my dad, really, I thought if we could go in as chairmen, and he could take all the credit and I could do all the work, then why not?'

Hunt had been in post for around a year when the game at the Boleyn Ground took place, and it had certainly been a busy 12 months, with a change of team management after the departure of Julian Dicks and the appointment of Marc Nurse, as well as a complete overhaul of the squad, including the departure of the long-serving captain Stacey Little. Added to that were organisational frustrations.

'Nobody really knew where anything was. Apparently we had a minibus, but nobody had the keys or indeed knew where the minibus was. It was all information gathering. In a small organisation, you don't have very good succession planning – one person leaves, they forget stuff, there was no password for the Facebook account, and not sure about the Twitter account, and the website was just a whole new world. It was just people clinging together – behind the scenes it wasn't very strongly structured at all, financial or organisational. That's my strength, so I spent a year worrying about that plus having fun on the media side, encouraging people. We were run by two people, maybe three, and now we're probably run by 20 or 30 people.

'We had some massive splits, and arguments, and chaos, and crazy things happened this season; I don't know whether that's all the bad stuff out in the first season or whether or not that's a typical season. I'll know next year. There have certainly been some interesting challenges. So far we've ridden them all and what doesn't kill you makes you stronger. In the summer, my father's press release when we got appointed said we would review and change everything.

'I don't think we expected to do it in the first six months, but that's effectively what happened. In any organisation it'll ruffle feathers when you start looking at things; people started jumping before they were pushed, you can't tell what causes the other. The way to deal with that is just to steer a steady course. There'll always be another game, there'll always be another season, people come and go, players come and go, so you just sit there and just wait.'

Hunt was pleased to see the development of a core fanbase as well, and has encouraged them to organise themselves independently of the club.

'It's important for them to be completely independent of us and criticise us if we do wrong, because we need the feedback of fans,' he said. 'I'm trying to encourage a very strong fan club that has the right to tell us what to do, because I'm too busy making sure we actually get the game on and the money is there and everything else – sometimes you just spread yourself too thinly, so I've encouraged lots of independence from different groups, and so far it's worked fairly well. I think I've kept everyone pretty much on board.'

Hunt hoped for a more settled season to come, and chose to formulate the chaotic first year of his tenure as 'an enormous pre-season'.

Leyton Orient – in their old yellow and green kit – return to the field against Eastbourne

Leyton Orient celebrate winning the Mayor's Cup (photo courtesy of Asif Burhan)

Goaldiggers' substitutes watch the action

Goaldiggers pose for a team photo

Goaldiggers coach Ruby gives the half-time team talk

Goaldiggers coach Ruby presents the player of the match medal to Fleur

*The Tottenham players line up for a
picture with their families and friends*

Tottenham beat Cardiff in extra-time of the FAWPL Cup Final

The players assess the Aggborough pitch before the WPL Cup Final

The champagne on offer for the victors, alongside the water necessary for a warm afternoon at Aggborough

Sheffield's development team prepare for a Birmingham free kick

'The plans in place for next year are astonishing compared with this season in terms of player recruitment. Last year [in pre-season] we played a couple of village sides and beat them 16-0 by way of preparation because it was all organised very hurriedly; we had, very late, Julian Dicks being headhunted by the main club – that caused us all sorts of issues. This season we're about to announce a tour of Holland, with FC Twente and other major names. We've got a very exciting pre-season with Super League sides, got some very interesting discussions going on with some major players, and I'm looking at the finances of putting people on to paid contracts and things like that – all part of the long plan. When we hired Marc Nurse it was always a two-year plan, so before we know it we're into year two. With a bit of support from West Ham as well, and the fanbase, hopefully we'll have a very interesting season.'

West Ham's new home from the summer of 2016 is the Olympic Stadium, built for the 2012 Games, and in the eyes of the public somewhat controversially converted to a 60,000-seater ground. Hunt was already planning to organise a game there at the showpiece stadium, and was hopeful that it would be possible.

'It's not that difficult – it's more about the expense,' he said. 'If we can guarantee enough people are there, and I need to work out the exact costs, if we can put it on, I think we will.'

Life at the bottom

GRASSROOTS football clubs always find themselves strapped for cash. Once kit is bought, pitches are hired and nets are hung, there's little left over from the players' weekly subs.

With all the money swilling about in the men's professional game, some of its sponsors have started to glance a little further down the pyramid and realised that their megabucks might be better spent elsewhere.

Beer company Budweiser, a sponsor of the FA Cup, partnered up with the FA and the Football Foundation to launch the Club Futures programme, a grassroots support scheme. One particular innovation is the Dream Goal competition – a hunt for the greatest amateur goals from across the country, which was relaunched at the start of 2016.

The lucky few got their goals analysed on television by former Liverpool players Jamie Carragher and Jamie Redknapp alongside broadcaster Ed Chamberlin – with the winner picking up £50,000 for their club, and the runners-up getting £10,000.

Women's teams were encouraged to enter in 2016, with former England captain Faye White taking on the role of ambassador to promote the competition and women's grassroots football.

'With this campaign, there's been more women's goals entered than last year, so that's a good sign that the game is growing and being recognised,' she said.

For the previous two years, a woman's goal had been nominated for the Puskas Award – FIFA's goal of the year prize – with Stephanie Roche and Carli Lloyd both gaining recognition on a global level for their skill. The Dream Goal competition offers an opportunity for amateur women players' goals to be seen on a national platform – alongside men.

'It's good that the women's game is growing enough to be recognised, included and considered for awards like that [the Puskas], and this Dream Goal competition as well,' said White. 'It shows the quality of the ladies' teams as well – some goals are crackers, scored equally in men's and women's football.

'The main reason behind the Budweiser Dream Goal campaign is to put money back in to clubs. It's good that the women's teams can be included as well – put their goals in and have that analysis of their goals if they're picked out. It's good that there's that prize fund – it shows that investment which is important at grassroots, on both.

'There's still a lot of work to be done in the women's game, allowing more clubs to grow and the facilities they have, and this will help.'

White was honest that there was a problem at grassroots level simply because of the amount of time and money it took to run a club well, whether it was for men or women.

'The teams have the same struggles,' she said. 'With grassroots football it's always based around volunteers as well, and then obviously it's those facilities that clubs are trying to establish and improve. Grassroots clubs are important for the local community as well, just to make sure that the national game continues to grow on both fronts. That kind of investment can make a lot of difference.'

White herself had begun her playing career at a time when the women's game, even at its highest level, was firmly amateur.

'When I started I was having to pay to play, carrying the nets to put up on the goals and things like that,' she recalled. 'That happens on Sundays in the men's and women's leagues up and down the country.'

She admitted with a smile that she couldn't help but covet the facilities the elite players had in England in the wake of the 2015 Women's World Cup.

'I'm a bit envious when I walk into the changing rooms and they've got their own little area!' she said, referring to the new hub built by Arsenal for the women's team. 'I would have loved to have had this. I had the best at my time, but it's just good to see the game keep growing and the investment that goes in.'

※ ※ ※ ※ ※

Running a football club takes time, money and a lot of hard graft. Even at professional level, where there are resources available – financial and personnel – it is not a simple matter. Starting a club from scratch at grassroots level and putting in the leg work to find facilities, recruit staff and players, and manage the fixture list is even tougher.

Fleur Cousens has done that twice. A football fan since childhood, as a little girl she played at the Arsenal soccer schools – until she turned ten, and was no longer able to participate in mixed teams.

'I loved it so much,' she recalled. 'We were all at the same standard and suddenly they said, "Oh, no, you're a girl, you can't play any more."'

Disappointed, she threw herself into other sports instead, but never found the same connection with swimming or tennis as she had with football. When she went to university in Edinburgh, she found herself envying the young men having a kickaround in the parks, and wondered if she could set up somewhere for women to give football a go as well.

'When I was in Australia, for my study abroad year from uni, for some reason it was just easier to play,' she said. 'Everyone would be like, "Oh, let's go and play," and go outside and have a kickaround. I got back into the swing of it, and from then I got more and more disheartened – but also angry that I wasn't playing just because of the fact that I'm a woman.

'So I decided to start up a team when I came back to Edinburgh for my final year. It started off as quite a small thing. I just wanted more women to get involved and for it to be not a sport which isn't an option just because you're a woman, basically.'

Fleur's club – the entertainingly-entitled 99 Problems But A Pitch Ain't One – was more successful than she ever imagined, and she decided to bring the concept back to London after she graduated. Her new club, Goaldiggers, have around 60 fully paid-up members plus a waiting list of about 30 – all women seeking a team to train with and play for in a reasonably central location within the capital.

That is tougher to find than one might imagine. Space in central London is at a premium – and the few pitches that there are incur extremely high hire costs. Although Cousens tried to gain some funding from the FA, the development officers in charge of supporting grassroots clubs were so overworked that it took them seven months to get back to her, by which time she had already managed to find somewhere to play as well as got hold of basic equipment. At a time when she should have been job-hunting, she was spending her time ringing round sports centres to find a pitch on which her team could train, and potential sponsors to fund the hire.

'There are so many obstacles for women playing football – there are SO many obstacles,' she emphasised. 'There are more obstacles when you're in London – with finance, and space, and time of travel. All I want is to minimise those obstacles, basically.

'So many boys growing up, it's part of their routine to play, it's part of their routine to pay ten pounds a week to go and play five-a-side, they wouldn't blink an eye at that. That's what they've been brought up doing, but none of my friends would be ready to do that, because they first need to understand what's behind football. They need a push – and they can't be turned away by finance.'

Cousens persuaded a local pub to sponsor the team, which enabled them to buy kits. Each player also pays a small membership fee to keep the club running and to pay for the entry fees into a local indoor five-a-side league. Even so, at the start of 2016, they were still struggling for money; with so many members, they had got two teams in the same league so that more people would have a chance to play.

'We're hugely in debt,' she admitted. The club's funding sub-committee had recently organised a successful crowdfunding campaign, raising £1,000, but even so, that would only cover part of the costs for the rest of the year. Goaldiggers were also paying a small sum to their two coaches, who worked with them every Tuesday evening. There would always be one coach with whoever was competing in the match, and one running a training session for those who did not want to play.

That, to the outsider, would be what makes Goaldiggers special. Not all of their registered players were happy to play in competitive games. So many of them had come to the game as adults, and were not confident enough in their skills to ply them in a league. Yet all of them found themselves progressing as players – even if they were not expecting to.

May Robson, who was part of the original Edinburgh club before joining Goaldiggers as a founder member, had a similar tale to Cousens's. She was interested in sport as a child but never really found one to suit her. She even tried out a local football club, but did not quite settle. Then when she started to play five-a-side, she realised this was the sport for her.

'When I was younger, I quit a lot of things because I wasn't instantly good at it,' she confessed over a hot drink in a coffee shop just before heading to Tuesday night training. 'I can't believe how much I've improved. To be called a good player on this team is still a big shock to me; I was such a beginner. I still feel frustrated after every game: you want to be able to play better than you can.

'[There was] a total change in confidence that I found in Edinburgh, playing sport, and such pride in being able to play football. It's the holy grail, it's something we've never had access to and to be able to be a part of it is quite exciting. Watching my friends who have never played a team sport – I was always sporty and I always had that confidence that I could do sport – but loads of my friends who have never identified as sporty say, "I've got to stop saying to myself that I'm not somebody who can play sport. I am. I'm doing it."'

Yet these women – like many others at grassroots level, in small-sided games and 11-a-side – reported that they were dealing with huge obstacles that could conceivably put them off playing. It was not just money proving a problem, but explicit sexism. Sometimes it was cat-calling from passers-by; Cousens talked about some shouts directed at her while she was stretching her calves on the sidelines during training, adding, 'You go through that in what's supposed to be a safe space to play football.' Sometimes it was aggression or mockery from men's teams training nearby. Sometimes, and startlingly, it was scoffing from match officials about players' abilities and knowledge of the game; in those situations, the players seemed embarrassed about being abused in such a way, and were loath to take formal action.

Despite these experiences, Robson was hopeful that these attitudes would change from the top down; she wondered whether the perceptions of women's football at grassroots level would change as the elite game got more and more coverage and was taken more and more seriously. She thought back to attending the Women's FA Cup Final as a child, when players were resolutely amateur save for the bankrolled Fulham side (which lasted only three years as a fully professional team at the turn of the millennium), and the handful of people who showed up to watch; and then she compared that with her experience watching England play Bosnia at Ashton Gate just four months previously.

'That was wicked,' she enthused. 'I had an amazing time, there was loads of girls there, it was a really nice atmosphere. It is changing.'

Change is, however, a long and slow process.

※ ※ ※ ※ ※

Jane Watkinson was thinking back over her playing career. A talented footballer, she had first kicked a ball as a small child and never looked back. She played for her school team and was snapped up by a local centre of excellence.

One day she walked off in the middle of a match and gave up football.

'I just walked in the middle of the game,' she said. 'I went off the pitch and I never played until I was 21 or 22. I don't know. I started to just not really enjoy the game – it was just pressure.'

She was sitting in a cafe in Sheffield city centre alongside Jay Baker, and talking about the events that had led them to create AFC Unity – a women's football club founded in 2014 without ties to a men's team. More than that, it was launched with a very distinctive ethos – a commitment to social justice and feminism, principles that have often been shied away from in sport.

Baker, a Doncaster fan, had been involved in the supporters' trust movement, and both had worked in social enterprise for some years. He had been watching a game in which Watkinson was playing, and came up with the idea for a new style of club.

'I said could we not run our own club? Could we not run it as a social enterprise with a particular focus on doing social good as well as playing football in – I want to say a fair way, but that sounds a bit clichéd now, "Oh, fair play and respect!"' He laughed, referring to the governing bodies' initiatives to encourage good behaviour on the pitch. 'Just in a way that's rooted in the community just as all grassroots clubs are, but yes, that's how it came about.'

He turned to Watkinson.

'And your response was, first of all it was, "Have you taken leave of your senses?"'

They both laughed again.

'Yeah, it took a while for me to get on board!' agreed Watkinson. 'I mean, I loved the idea of it, it fits in with my ethos and the way I perceive football should be, and my own experiences. The key thing with this as well was I wanted it to be more fun, and not just about winning.'

With help from the FA, AFC Unity was up and running within a matter of months. Watkinson advertised in carefully-chosen local media – the idea was not necessarily to attract any player, but the right players, ones who would relish the opportunity to be part of a community project. AFC Unity is now a social enterprise in its own right, thanks to funding from a local scheme, and it has also received funding from South Yorkshire Sport to run sessions for women who are new to the sport or who simply do not want to play competitively. That operates alongside a five-a-side team in the local PowerLeague, and the 11-a-side first team, who play in the Sheffield and Hallamshire Women's County Football League.

Of course football is important, but for AFC Unity it is not everything; indeed, the 'AFC' stands not for 'Association Football Club', as it usually does, but 'Alternative Football Club'. They have decided to do things very differently from the start. Their vision has been set out on their website, 'AFC Unity envision a society where the football club plays an active role in its community, engaging and empowering women as positive role models, and using the sport to encourage unity, solidarity, and social cohesion.' They want to empower women, challenge stereotypes and all kinds of discrimination, and offer a vehicle for campaigning on important social issues; in the past year, they have been running a Football for Food project, encouraging donations to the 17 local food banks.

'After the first season, we sat down and we said, "Right, we have to define the aims, the values and the vision of the club,"' said Watkinson. 'On the "about us" page on the website, you'll see all that outlined. That was us sitting down and going, "We need to make this really clear and something that we can provide anybody that wants to be part of the club in any capacity."

'The Football for Food campaign was influenced by that as well: wanting to do something on game days that showed our alternative ethos. It's not just coming down and watching a game of football – can you donate some food as well which will go to food banks which then highlights food poverty locally? It was all about trying to make it all a little bit clearer – and we also wanted to do something a bit more.'

'Something socially radical, almost,' added Baker, who suggested that even in 2016 the idea of women's football has still been taken too lightly, and often treated as just a box-ticking exercise, an easy way to indicate interest in equality and diversity without too much effort. 'We want to say, "No, let's do more than that, something tangible." Jane's idea with food bank stuff: it's an actual outcome there and then, it's food and people need food, so it's an easy-to-understand concept.'

It has also had the effect of encouraging their players to become more politically engaged and more aware about what has been happening in communities – locally and around the world. Watkinson talked with animation about one player's increased interest in the news, and concluded, 'And it was awesome, that, somebody who's not really thought about that before suddenly becoming switched on because it's football connecting them to those issues.'

That has not meant that everyone has always necessarily been supportive of the AFC Unity ethos. Baker and Watkinson both talked about the abuse and the lower-level sarcasm that has been directed at them on social media, but also the aggressive attitudes of other teams and coaches – as well as difficult players within the AFC Unity set-up.

'It's weird,' said Watkinson. 'I do feel that we're judged by almost harsher standards because we try to do something different – I think people are always waiting to catch us out. People in the club itself, who have played for us, they do a similar kind of thing to other players from other teams, using the ethos against you, "It's democracy, can't I say what I want?" Or, "Unity – this isn't unity!" Oh my God, it isn't like your interests at the expense of everybody else, that's not what this club is about!'

'It's about making sure that people are aware the culture isn't just for them,' added Baker. 'It's not just about what they get out, it's about what they put in, it's about that collective spirit. It's important that everyone contributes to that. It's not just about, "Oh, I'll be accepted here." We keep that friendliness and that kind of ethos going.'

That welcoming atmosphere has been integral to bringing the squad together.

'We've had quite a lot of players who've said they wouldn't have played football, wouldn't have stayed involved or never played for a club, if we hadn't have been here,' explained Watkinson. She pointed to her own experience, dropping out of organised football as a teenager because she did not get on with the manager and felt she could not flourish in a regimented centre of excellence set-up.

'We have at least one in our team as well who was at the centre of excellence and she stopped as well. She was in the uni team and she quit that as well. She loves it here now, she's really good, but I think you either suit it or you don't, and there's a small amount of people who suit that [centre of excellence].'

Baker wondered whether coaching methods in England were still developing, and moving towards a system where individuals were allowed to develop, and Watkinson agreed.

'[At the centre of excellence] you didn't really feel like you had a lot of freedom to do what you wanted to do,' she recalled. 'I was awful. Just thinking about how I played back then, I looked like I couldn't kick a ball, because every time I had the ball I was just so scared to do something. Better to do nothing and not mess it up than do something and then get told that you messed up.'

The club's coaching and playing style encourages positivity, about which Baker was very enthusiastic. He spoke with a heavy dose of irony about his experience as a man coaching an explicitly feminist football team, and his philosophy of working with them.

'I always think of it as the perfect political analogy: our team has got all of these unique individuals all working in a different style to each of their team-mates, but it all works and I love that. Everyone gets to express themselves, and they don't need men telling them what to do all the time, they have enough of that out there without coming to football! That's what I always say, 'I'm just here to guide you all, and someone's got to take the rap for the formation being wrong, and that's what I'm here for.' That's it, that's all it is, I'm just the scapegoat.'

He was evidently joking, but the club's positive philosophy had proved successful so far, encouraging entertaining football with plenty of goals. They referred to 'training exercises' rather than the more military-sounding 'drills', and made sure that the coach's feedback to players was never criticism and never directed at a single player within the group.

'Our approach to coaching is 100 per cent positivity at all times,' he said. 'A team can develop somebody without being negative – saying, "Oh, you did that really well last week." It's the way that you can frame things. Staying positive all the time in games and training: it sounds impossible until you try and do it, and actually it's really easy to be positive at all times.'

That gave them the idea for another community initiative on the theme of anti-bullying, tying in well to some workshops they had been running in local schools.

'It was so obvious we didn't really think of it until recently,' he said. Baker had seen first-hand some of the aggression that players from various teams had directed at their own colleagues, and he mentioned one who had later asked whether she could join AFC Unity instead, attracted to its positivity.

'It's astonishing to think you were part of that and you feel like you've got to be part of that, but you want to get out of that because you've got to do that to survive in that environment, toughen up and shout abuse at each other,' said Baker. '"Someone's shouting at me, I'll shout back at them."'

He was grateful that the AFC Unity players had adopted the club ethos and generally got on well, on and off the pitch.

'They're actually a fairly quiet team: they need to work on that sometimes in terms of verbal communication,' said Baker. 'The other downside of it, which is related to that, is that they're incredibly modest. We attract those kinds of players:

amazing players, centre of excellence players, absolutely incredible – none of them think they're particularly fabulous.

'So we had a 60 seconds of celebration at training on Monday, it was our last training session of the season. I said, "For 60 seconds, don't be modest. Instead of being modest and going, 'Oh, we don't want to upset the other team too much,' just 60 seconds of outlandish celebrations, just go for it, get it out of our systems, we're at the training ground, so it's fine, no one else can see it."

'It comes with being nice people, they're so modest. "You were amazing!" "Nah, I'm no good, I didn't play that well." You did! What's wrong with you?! The games are filmed now so they'll be able to see, I don't know how they'd be able to watch it and go no, I didn't play well.'

Watkinson suggested that female players have historically played the game in a fairer way than their male counterparts ('It seems to be played in a bit more mature way to the men's game,' she speculated), and Baker added that this attitude was reflected at the highest level of women's football – one of the reasons he encouraged the players to watch Women's Super League matches whenever they could.

'I say to go away and find someone who plays in your position in the WSL or something like that, so in that sense you can have positive female role models rather than comparing themselves to men all the time, and emulating men, and the cheating that goes along with the men's game,' he said.

They did both acknowledge that perhaps with increased investment into women's football, when results were becoming more and more important, the characteristics that had long been associated with the game could change. Even at their level, AFC Unity needed money just to keep running, not to mention roll out the community schemes they were planning.

Nourish, the cafe in which Baker and Watkinson were sitting, had agreed to sponsor the club for the 2016-16 season, receiving advertisements on the kit, the club website and social media in exchange for its money. The owners had been attracted to AFC Unity's focus on the community and social justice – principles they shared and encouraged through their healthy fast food. They had been asked to sponsor teams before, and had always turned it down.

'They said, "Okay, you play football, what else do you do?" And they were like, "We just play football,"' explained Baker.

Watkinson was pleased that the club could, in return, support an independent local business.

'It's also really good for us, healthy foods, so it connects to that as well,' she added.

They also had plans for expansion – a development side alongside the first team, more community sessions, including the continuation of the Football for Food work, and perhaps even their own ground at some point, which could be used as a hub for more projects.

Yet they were very aware of the paradox that even though football was not their sole motivator, they needed to do well on the pitch in order to be taken seriously – particularly as a women's club with no men's team with which to affiliate.

'That's a problem we might be faced with – it is quite unique, even locally. In all these three divisions one other team is exclusively for women only; all the others are tagged on, associated with a men's club,' admitted Baker.

'We wouldn't want to do that,' said Watkinson.

'If we were at a regional level, I think that would suit us – we're not getting too carried away,' said Baker. 'It's exclusively for women and is a women's club, but I do think we need to raise our profile as well so that we can do more in the community. If we're just rock bottom then that's rubbish, no one's going to be particularly fussed about it, "We're not going to listen to you, you're rubbish!" So it is important that you engage as well.'

Part of the AFC Unity vision says, 'If you are only about winning, when you lose it feels like you have nothing else left.' Baker and Watkinson were focused on results – but not those on the pitch. They were more pleased about their community work, about creating a unified squad.

'A lot of really good players find – this sounds really corny – but they find a home,' said Baker. 'They finally find somewhere to go where they can express themselves a bit and feel relaxed. It's a nice style, it's not an army camp, there won't be screaming and shouting – unless it's encouragement.'

And, of course, they were pleased about the club's bright future. A few weeks later, AFC Unity confirmed that they would be running a new 11-a-side team in 2016/17, the Jets – a hint of 'suffragette' in the name as a nod to the feminist founding principles – giving more players the chance of minutes on the pitch. A few days after that, they announced that they had rebranded their community coaching as 'Solidarity Soccer', retaining all their principles and adding in an emphasis on technology to make the sessions as interactive as possible.

After quitting football as a promising youngster, Watkinson had finally found her footballing home – somewhere where the game was important, but doing the right thing and doing good were both even more so.

'The community aspect of the club, and that's what we focus on, really,' she said, 'it's all anchored in how football can create social change – it's not just about football for football's sake.'

The future
is feminine?

ON 8 March every year is International Women's Day. FIFA, seeking to be ahead of the curve, held its Women's Football and Leadership conference in Zurich the day before, capitalising on the social media hashtags and coinciding with four of the international big-hitters competing in the SheBelieves Cup.

The snow was intermittent but the chilliness was constant throughout the city, famous for its beautiful views and spectacular lake. FIFA's headquarters, referred to corporately as 'Home of FIFA', is a steep uphill walk from the city centre and situated near the zoo. Security is, unsurprisingly, high. While the guests of honour, including tennis legend Billie Jean King and USA's World Cup winner Abby Wambach, were shuttled from their hotel in one bus and welcomed through the main entrance, the other delegates were driven in another and entered the building through an underground car park.

Those other delegates might not have been invited to speak, but there were some famous names in there – former players and coaches from around the world, representatives from member football associations, unions and tournaments, as well as several journalists keen to report the discussions at the start of a new era for FIFA.

The organisation's public image had been damaged hugely in the preceding 12 months, with allegations about criminal misconduct thrown at many of the organisation's hierarchy. Although most of them had stepped down, their names were still inscribed on a plaque near the building's entrance; clearly newly-elected FIFA president Gianni Infantino had not had time to get his feet under the table since his appointment the previous week.

He was on show, though, and welcomed all the guests at the start of the day. He acknowledged – as perhaps one might expect in a room dominated by female experts on football – that the game needed to welcome the contribution of women at all levels, including on the executive committee with overall responsibility for the sport's progress across the globe; indeed, he wondered aloud whether FIFA's current problems would have snowballed so far had it had more women involved in governance. He referred to his four daughters, and his desire to create a better, fairer world for them.

Infantino reiterated, however, that his manifesto for change could not be implemented solely through his will.

'Alone I cannot do anything. I will need all of you,' he told the room, and by extension the thousands of people watching the lives streaming across the world.

Billie Jean King was the invited keynote speaker, talking about her career fighting for equality and against the discrimination endemic in sport, and inspiring her audience, steeped in a game still dominated by white men. She talked of her experience joining a tennis club, and realising that she was surrounded by white faces; she talked of her experience fighting for equal prize money for women tennis players, collaborating with her peers and taking collective action, and emphasised that she wanted elite female athletes to be paid for their sporting excellence, not for the way they looked.

This comment was particularly incisive; some attendees from the world of the media had been overheard earlier talking about the need for female footballers to look like they had 'made an effort' with their appearance on the field of play if they ever wanted to get a decent pay packet or wider media coverage.

'Women are told to be happy with the crumbs,' she said. 'We deserve the cake, the icing, and the cherry on top also.'

There was English interest in the first panel event of the day, with Asisat Oshoala of Liverpool Ladies talking about how she fought prejudice to become a professional footballer, and Barbara Slater, the BBC's director of sport, discussing how her corporation covers women's football, with particular reference to the 2015 Women's World Cup.

'Half were introduced to the game on television for the first time in 2015,' she enthused. 'An interesting thing coming from the split of the audience that watched in 2015, 67 per cent of that audience was men, 33 per cent were women, so there is an enormous audience of women who haven't yet all been won round. I think that's interesting because our figures for the men's World Cup, you've got a pretty even gender split in viewership.'

Some might consider those statistics unsurprising. It is well known that England has inconsistent media coverage of women's international competition, and a small and new domestic league aired on a subscription-only digital channel since its inception.

Add to that the confusion around the fixture list and the lack of regular days and kick-off time for matches, and it is simple to conclude that one of the problems with women's football in England is you already have to know what's going on to be able to watch it; you have to make educated guesses so that you can seek it out.

That means that women's football is not stamping its imprint on the public profile or reaching out to convert non-football fans; it is attracting only the people who already love the sport.

Slater did acknowledge that the comparatively low viewing figures for women's football would put broadcasters under commercial pressure.

'The TV schedules are incredibly competitive,' she admitted. 'It is difficult to take a programme off the air that may be watched by six or seven million and put a programme on that's watched by two million. I think maybe we're in a very fortunate position with the BBC as it's a public service broadcaster and I do think we would have made space in the schedules because I think there is a real momentum.

'I think women's football at the moment is very much a flag-bearer for the whole of women's sport. There is an investment that sometimes needs to be made to build for the future, and I would just go back to the figures and compare the European Championships, again many of those matches were in a reasonable peak time, and the audience which doubled in two years. I think that's a great achievement.'

Slater, however, was keen to emphasise what a great event she thought the World Cup was – and urged similar quality tournaments in future, arguing that this would trickle down to the domestic leagues.

'There was a tremendous sense of momentum [in Canada],' she said. 'I would just have to pay tribute to the quality of the organisation of the World Cup in Canada, the quality of the coverage, the crowds. This was a superb event. If you're going to show something to audiences at home, it's got to look brilliant on the screen and it's got to have a fantastic atmosphere. I think that's only achieved in partnerships between broadcasters and governing bodies, between sponsors coming together to create a great event, a great experience, and I think that creates a springboard for the future. You try to concentrate on a virtuous cycle. Success breeds success breeds success.'

As an example, she pointed to the way that the FA and broadcasters had worked together to produce live coverage of

England's friendly against Germany at Wembley in November 2014, creating a spectacular occasion with thousands of fans, 'It was just a fabulous occasion of choosing a moment and making it fabulous.'

Perhaps more significantly for fans of the game in England, who have long complained about being unable to follow the team if they have an away match even in major championship qualification, Slater explained that sometimes decisions to air matches are based on predicted attendances as well as the expected footage quality for just these reasons.

'We've had conversations with the FA where we've had coverage coming in from abroad and we have mutually decided not to televise, because there's been no crowd and there's been nervousness about the quality of the coverage,' she said. 'I think it's finding more moments and it's making sure those moments are a wonderful shop window and showcase. Audiences don't want to watch sport played if there's no atmosphere and there's no crowds, and I think that's where it's a partnership.'

Fellow panellist Abby Wambach, a World Cup winner with the USA, asked her whether the crowds would come without the media coverage, leading Slater to reiterate, 'It's a virtuous cycle,' and then add, 'But I think you want to find high-quality moments that are winning their place, and then I think you leave your audience wanting even more. For those people who for the first time watched a women's football match [in 2015], a lot of them said they would go on to follow [the women's game]. We actually saw quite a burst in the UK of attendances as well, flowing from the success of the World Cup. This will change over time, but I would say that at the moment the right thing is to focus on really brilliant showcase moments, show off the women's game at its very best, then the regularity hopefully comes.'

Again, some might wonder if Slater's prediction was founded in fact. Glossy elite international showpiece events might be pleasing to the eye of a casual viewer, but it seems unlikely that this will trickle down to domestic level – even the top end of the domestic pyramid. Indeed, though WSL1 teams saw a bit of a boost after 2015's Women's World Cup, with fans wanting to see the Lionesses they had enjoyed watching on television, WSL2 attendances stayed static, unable to capitalise on the marketing ploy of luring an audience with the promise of international stars.

The difference between an event held in an Olympic-size and -standard stadium and a match played in a non-league ground is stark. From the audience, Australian football administrator Heather Reid spoke a great deal of sense about the need for member associations and broadcasters to invest in a sport they want people to watch; however, it seemed unlikely that her words, calling for capital outlay, would be heeded.

A change of pace followed, with an inspirational addition from Professor Michael Kimmel of Stony Brook University. A sociologist and sports consumer rather than a sports researcher, and a self-defined male feminist, his speech was intended to open up a discussion on how men could be encouraged to embrace and promote gender equality.

Perhaps the most eagerly awaited speaker was Moya Dodd; once a Matilda, the nickname for Australia's team, then a very successful lawyer, then elected to FIFA's executive committee. She had spent her tenure thus far arguing for greater gender parity within the governance structures, and the reforms passed by FIFA the week before were a step towards that, guaranteeing at least six women on the executive committee, and an obligation to support women's football as well as women in football.

She took the opportunity to address Infantino directly and put some direct proposals to him – including a suggestion for a women's World Club Championship.

'We don't need to think about women as a problem that needs to be addressed…we're part of the solution,' she told him, adding, 'All the horrible things you hear about FIFA, none of them are about women's football.'

Infantino was obviously taken aback slightly to be put on the spot to such a degree, but reiterated his support for Dodd's ideas – albeit adding the caveat that FIFA's problems were so immense that it had a number of other priorities that needed to be addressed. However, he did agree, 'Women's football and women in football is a priority – it's part of the solution for the future of football.'

It would be an uphill struggle. While this was all happening, the *Daily Mail* reported that the FA of Wales had taken the visiting representatives attending the International Football Association Board meeting off to Swansea to watch the Premier League clash with Norwich. Meanwhile, their womenfolk were taken off to a cookery class rather than heading to the game.

※ ※ ※ ※ ※

The FA had its own plans, launching two new girls' and women's football initiatives almost simultaneously.

First, the Girls' Football Weeks were announced; they had been incredibly successful in 2015, beyond the FA's expectations, resulting in a 2016 repeat. The idea was to combine FA-endorsed coaching sessions with schools' enthusiasm for girls' football, offering resources and session plans for teachers who might want to help their pupils get into the game but did not know where to start.

'When you start something like this, it's hard to know what the take-up will be, really, so we've gone for a 20 per cent increase [target] this year,' said the FA's Kelly Simmons. 'We want to see more schools and more girls get involved, but last year was fantastic. I guess it's all part of what was a very special year for women's football. The Lionesses were doing well with building profile in the run-up to the World

Cup, with the unbeaten run; the Women's FA Cup Final was coming to Wembley; WSL was getting a lot more coverage, so I think it's a lot more factors, really – not just the World Cup. I just think it's all part of the increasing profile and interest in the women's and girls' game.'

Then the WSL announced a Sister Clubs project, partnering with local clubs and providing coaching, facilities and player appearances along with experiences such as the opportunity to be a matchday mascot or ballgirl.

'We want young girls to start to play football, enjoy it, and enjoy it for life, and as part of that to follow their local club and those role models to inspire them to keep playing,' explained Simmons. 'So it makes total strategic sense, really, for WSL clubs to partner with local girls' clubs. Arsenal have already run a scheme similar to this, and we've worked with them to replicate it across the other clubs and it's worked really well, and I think there's some great benefits to be had on both sides of local girls' clubs partnering with a WSL club – the girls coming along to support the team and see top-level women's football, but also the support the clubs can give those girls' teams, whether that's coaching or promotional events or profile.

'If you're Arsenal, you haven't got room for every girl that wants to play for Arsenal, but if you've got a partnership with loads of local girls' teams, you can be feeding girls through into your community programme. There's so many benefits of working together, it makes absolute sense – get really good strong partnerships and support those local girls' clubs.'

Simmons was incredibly enthusiastic about the success of the WSL and the career avenues it was opening up, showing girls and young women that they could indeed be professional footballers in England if they wanted to be – a far cry from just a few years previously.

'I remember some research we did with Women in Sport, and one of the reasons why girls dropped out of football was that they and their parents couldn't see any career for them, whereas with boys if they were quite a good footballer, there was always this hope they'd get this ticket to fame and wealth. On the girls' side that wouldn't be possible so they weren't really encouraged to keep playing,' she said.

'We did some work where we promoted all the different careers you could have if you were interested in football, Jacqui Oatley played football and became a famous football commentator, and there were a number of people in there coaching or working in the commercial sector and there were all sorts of different moves.

'What we were saying at that time was you might not have a career as a footballer, but there's a whole industry you could work in, and use your love and interest in playing football. Now you can add to that playing. You can be Steph Houghton. You can travel the world for the Lionesses. You can play for Man City, or Chelsea, or whoever, and be a professional footballer, and I think that's hugely powerful in inspiring girls to play.'

*% *% *% *% *%

On a more local level, one community organisation in Sheffield was launching its own Female Football Festival, running throughout March and encompassing International Women's Day celebrations.

Football Unites, Racism Divides (FURD) is based not far from Bramall Lane, the home of Sheffield United; it has a small building with offices and classrooms, enabling it to offer workshops and training, and it has a set of football pitches outside.

Its ethos is that football can create community cohesion and challenge prejudices. Its focus – as per its name – might be on racism, but it also promotes opportunities for girls and women to get involved in the game as well.

The festival concluded, coincidentally, with events on the pitch, and the finals of the FA People's Cup, held in Sheffield. FURD's female veterans entered a team, although they were not necessarily expecting too much success.

'Last year, I was already thinking it would be good to stage our own veterans' match,' said FURD's development officer Ruth Johnson, a few weeks after the tournament. 'It's a way of getting more older players engaged, maybe; there's nowhere left to play if you can't take the pace. I heard about the People's Cup, that there was a female veterans' section, and I never heard of any such thing before, so I thought we should enter it, support it.'

They did – and found themselves doing surprisingly well, making it to the final. Johnson's colleague, volunteer Sarah Choonara, was part of the veterans' team as well.

'We didn't know what to expect, we haven't played together as a team, so we haven't got a history of thinking, "This is what we're like and this is what we've achieved." To make the final was really exciting, a massive and unexpected surprise,' she said.

Their goalkeeper for the majority of the tournament was Sharon Leech, who, as a pianist, was extremely wary about protecting her hands – but also desperate to win.

'One of the Crawley Old Girls said to me, "Oh, it's the taking part, we're not in it to win it,"' she recalled. 'In the back of my mind I was thinking, "I want to win it!"'

Her team-mates laughed.

They agreed that the further they had progressed in the tournament, the more they had wanted to win it. Even so, they also enjoyed the day's atmosphere, which was incredibly supportive – despite the teams meeting for the first time that day.

As one player put it, 'If they were a female veteran we were hugging and high-fiving – even on the pitch as we were going on to play against each other.'

'After the first match, we were hearing what the other results were, and I was thinking, "If they lost to them, we beat them, so we could beat them as well,"' said one player. 'That's when we started thinking we could do something. It became apparent that the ones to beat were the Hackney Jurassics.'

One of the Hackney Jurassics' players was Francesca Cagetti, of Leyton Orient, who had moved to England permanently in 2006 after a playing career in Italy and a short spell at Chelsea before their explosion into the big-time. Now the managing director of her own ice cream firm, she was approaching the age of 40 and seemed wildly entertained that the FA People's Cup also marked her first appearance in an official veterans' team.

'To play at this level is an achievement!' she laughed. 'I wouldn't think it. I started when I was 21, so late compared to my team-mates, but I'm still playing – at a good level, at Leyton Orient with a new team. It's very exciting. I'm very pleased.'

Her playing career might have only started formally in her 20s but she did kick a ball around as a child. 'I always played football when I was little,' she recalled. 'I started playing when I was 21 in a proper team; before, it was with some friends or on the street. A team were training near my house, so I thought, "Okay, let me see, let me try." So I was part of the team, and from there my career started. I went to Serie C and Serie B and then Serie A, and then I came to England and played for Chelsea Ladies for a year, went back to Italy and finished the season with my old team, and then I moved for good here.

'I played a few years in five-a-side because when you move you need to find a job, and it's not that easy, especially when you come from a small village in Italy and you find London a completely different world! Then I started playing 11-a-side again with Hackney and then Kikk, which is now Leyton Orient. So I'm still playing – I'm still here.'

Perhaps it was not surprising that, with such a background, the Jurassics beat the FURD team quite easily in the final. The runners-up were not too disappointed.

'I was just bowled over by the fact we were in the final,' admitted one player. 'For me, that was amazing. I would have loved to have won it, but I was happy we were in the final.'

Cagetti, meanwhile, had enjoyed the experience of playing in the FA People's Cup, even if the standard had not been as high as she would have liked.

'It was an easy job,' she joked. 'We had them, and we won. It was more about the atmosphere and everything. This was the first time they had the over-35s ladies [competition] but I'm sure that in following years it will be more difficult, the level is probably going to grow. But, you know, we won it, so that's good anyway!'

Cagetti was excited at the prospect of match highlights being broadcast on the BBC's *Football Focus* programme for the rest of the country to see – but was already thinking about next season.

'I would like to play for as long as I can,' she said. 'I just stopped for a year because I had an injury to my ankle. At the moment I'm okay. I can do another season. I think.'

Despite finishing second, the FURD team were the main focus of the BBC highlights.

'I think we epitomised what the spirit of the competition was – taking part for the fun of it,' said Johnson.

They were already thinking about next year's tournament – and how they could prepare better. They had received invitations from some of the other competing teams to visit for a friendly match or two, and other players were interested in joining the squad.

'I'd like us to stay in a team and do the serious training to do one better next time because I think we do have good discipline,' said one player.

Johnson and Choonara were also thinking about how they could build on FURD's festival, to reach a wider audience in 2017.

'I think it's really raised the profile of what FURD does for girls' and women's football,' said Choonara.

Johnson agreed, adding that the timing of the People's Cup finals in the city fitted in perfectly with their plans.

'It was a complete coincidence – couldn't have ended better,' she said, before correcting herself with an ironic grin, 'Well, it could have ended better, obviously, but it was a great finale.'

The big kick-off

I T was a mild early spring Wednesday evening in Hertfordshire when Arsenal welcomed Reading to Meadow Park for their first game of the WSL season. The brand-new season tickets were swiped at the turnstiles, slightly sticking; the loyalty cards, rewarding consistent attendance, were dished out. It was warm and dry enough to stand on either of the terraces, positioned behind each goal; it was still not warm enough to sit on the cold concrete without placing a protective jacket or blanket there first.

Before the match, officials wandered round the stands, notebook and pen in hand, to ask fans some questions about why they watched women's football, evidently in an effort to steer future marketing strategy – how long have you been watching, do you watch the men's game too, what impact do you think the World Cup had, what could we do to attract more fans to women's football?

Dozens of girls and young women were watching along with their own club-mates, some welcoming the teams on to the pitch with flags, others acting as impromptu ball girls, the rest just enjoying the match, along with 1,200 others – a fine crowd for the first game of the season, particularly in midweek.

Reading, in their debut WSL1 game, battled hard, but they were no match for the sheer class of Arsenal. Pedro

Martinez Losa had named a side strong enough to beat the WSL1 newcomers but with an eye to the next match, five days later at Manchester City's Academy Stadium. That being the case, he had a substitutes' bench consisting of six full internationals, demonstrating the strength in depth he could boast in the squad.

Midway through the second half, one of those subs began to warm up and strip off her tracksuit, ready to come on. Two little girls, no older than eight, saw the activity on the touchline, and immediately started to race over there, as one whispered with awe, 'It's NATALIA!' The work of inspiring the next generation had evidently already taken root.

※ ※ ※ ※ ※

One day later, two WSL2 fixtures were scheduled, and both kicked off late. Millwall Lionesses were travelling to Oxford United; Aston Villa were visiting Everton. The day was Maundy Thursday, the day before the long Easter weekend, and the away sides both got caught up in intense traffic. Everton put their kick-off back by half an hour; Oxford's match was delayed by a whole hour, meaning it did not come to a conclusion much before 11pm. That one was certainly worth waiting for, though, finishing with a 5-3 win to the visitors, including a fabulously-taken lobbed goal from Ashlee Hincks.

Millwall had had a close season of change, with new coach Rebecca Sawiuk replacing Dan Mlinar, plus a new administrative hierarchy as Hannah Burnett-Kirk took over as general manager as well as coaching in the centre of excellence. The set-up was becoming slowly more professional, with players taking jobs coaching or within the club to enable a more flexible schedule which allowed them to train and play without financial losses. They also revelled in access to facilities at The New Den, legendary home of the men's team – not just for training a couple of times a week, but also for matches.

Burnett-Kirk was grateful for that kind of support. A digital marketer by trade, she was combining communications with administration with her football knowledge, and finding that she had to stay as absolutely organised as possible.

'There's so much to do,' she said, listing all the different companies and organisations with whom she had to liaise. 'You'll probably have a list of 20 things to do, and it's just about making sure you remember all those things and it's all ticked off and everything runs smoothly on matchdays. It's such a varied job, especially if you combine it with the marketing stuff as well. It's a big role, a very important role – and the support of the men's club helps quite a lot to be honest.'

Burnett-Kirk shared an office with Millwall's marketing team, and worked closely with the press office to ensure maximum publicity for any events focusing on the Lionesses; the women's team even got their kit laundered by the club.

'It's very conjoined,' she explained, 'and obviously we're treated the same as the men, which is fantastic. They're a League 1 club so it's not like they're Premier League, or Arsenal or Liverpool or Chelsea, but at the same time they're striving for bigger things, and we're striving for bigger things too.'

She knew her task over the coming months would centre around attracting more people to games. As a general rule, Millwall Lionesses played their home games at The Den, just as the men did – except for when there was a fixture clash, as there was on Easter Sunday. The men got first dibs, and the women ended up playing at Dartford. Burnett-Kirk was extremely focused on ensuring that fans were kept informed and engaged.

'It's building a relationship with the local community and local schools – getting young girls playing football, getting them into football, getting them close to the Millwall Lionesses first team, making sure season ticket holders and the fans are happy. Basically, it's bums on seats and making sure fan engagement is top notch. You go to Arsenal and Chelsea, there's great fan engagement – and we have to try to be as good as them really.'

※ ※ ※ ※ ※

Sheffield's development side didn't get to use the Coach and Horses ground, the Home of Football, for their Easter Sunday fixture against Birmingham City. Instead, they relocated about a mile across Dronfield, to Gosforth Fields, a community sports complex with a full-size 3G pitch available.

The cold wind gusted across the new-build residential estate surrounding the pitches as the dark clouds scurried over the sky. The glum weather did not, however, affect the mood of the players, clustering an hour and a half before kick-off in the balcony sports bar, overlooking the turf where they would be playing during the afternoon.

Clutching their bottles of water and dressed in their Sheffield tracksuits, they were waiting to get into the changing rooms, currently occupied by a group of youngsters who had been playing during the morning. The Sheffield squad looked smart but very young as they took their seats around the bar tables, chattering and catching up with their team-mates, while the Birmingham squad, more subdued after their coach journey, gathered in a corner.

As soon as the changing rooms were empty, the bar cleared as the players stampeded downstairs. One took a last look at the big screen showing the previous night's MLS match between New York City and New England Revolution, where one of the visiting players had just been sent off.

'That were never a red card,' she declared, and left.

Outside, the team's coaching staff were preparing, laying cones across the turf ready for the warm-up. They were newly in place after Zoe Johnson had been promoted from development team coach to the first team, but Helen Mitchell was still there overseeing everything.

'Our new development team coach is from Bristol, but he's moved up to Sheffield about a year ago,' she explained. 'He's been out in America for about three years coaching girls' football. He's back here working for the county FA in the day and just done some work with [Sheffield] Wednesday academy boys. He doesn't see a pathway with the boys because he's not an ex-pro and that's the way the academy system with the boys' side is going – you might be the best coach but if you haven't played before professionally, then they're rushing ex-players through. He's thought there might be more of a pathway in the women's game. He's great, really enthusiastic.'

As Mitchell made her way down to the side of the pitch, new first-team coach Zoe Johnson walked into the bar. She had only got home a few hours previously, travelling back with her team after their draw away at Bristol, and had lost 60 precious minutes of sleep with the clocks going forward. Nevertheless, she decided to travel to Dronfield to watch the development side, who had been her charges until recent weeks.

'I do get told I'm a little bit biased towards the development squad – some of the first-team squad say, "Oh, you've got your blinkers on when it comes to the development squad,"' she grinned, 'and I think it's just because they've been a big part of the last few years. The development team has always been close to my heart, and I think it has to be. It's vital, especially at a club like Sheffield FC, we've not got all the ability to go out and buy new players, so it's crucial to have a strong development squad. I think we have. They've come in this season and took [the league] by storm, they've beaten teams like Manchester City and Liverpool, not just once but twice. It is very important to me that everything is right in the development squad so that when we do need the players for the first team, they can step up, and it's not a big financial cost to the club.'

When Mick Mulhern had taken over as manager, he asked Johnson, with three years of experience at the club, to be his assistant, which came as a surprise to her.

'Within a couple of weeks of Mick being there, he had a chat with me and said, "I'd like you to come and be my assistant," and at first I was like, "Well, you don't really know me yet,"' she said. 'For the club, it has to be the right decision – right for everybody involved, right for Mick. I said, "You've got to work with me first, hold fire," and he was like, "All right, just to let you know you're one of the people I'm really keen to get on board," and I said, "Thank you very much, that's a big compliment, let's see how things happen in the next couple of weeks."

'A couple of weeks went by and he said, "No, I definitely want you to come up from development manager – is that what you want?" And it was hard because of course it's what I want. I want to work in first-team football, I'm not going to pass up an opportunity like that – but at the same time I'd brought in the majority of those players; some of them had been here for a while but this pre-season we had an overhaul and brought in quite a lot of new players, so I felt like I'd made promises and I owed them a lot.

'To leave them halfway through a season, at the end of November, that's not really fair, not the right thing to do, but it's the big picture for the club as well as for me personally. I had to make that step, so I agreed everything with Mick and we went from there, really.'

Yet by the second week of March – a fortnight before the start of the WSL season – Mulhern had left Sheffield by mutual consent. Johnson was then called to a very surprising meeting.

'The club instantly asked me to attend a meeting and just said, "Look, we think you're the right person to take things forward. The girls buy into what you're about, they all respect you, we don't think there's anyone better – that's what the girls are going to buy into." I was a bit taken aback.'

Johnson decided that it was an offer she couldn't refuse, and has been reassured by the club's evident faith in her.

'I'm still young, I still want to learn. Am I still going to get to learn? I was looking forward to learning off Mick Mulhern and all his experience, but the club have given me their 100 per cent support. They've brought in someone else as well with an A Licence who's worked in football for a long time, so they've supported me and I can still learn as well, and the girls are happy – they know me well, they know what I'm about, they know what I expect from them, so really we're just perfect.'

At the age of 25, she was the youngest WSL manager in 2016 – and one of the few women in post as well. After eight years of coaching, at Preston North End and Blackburn Rovers as well as Sheffield, she was about to start working towards her UEFA A Licence, and had realised that she would need to reassess her commitments – especially bearing in mind she was also working full-time during the day.

'I'm a maintenance surveyor during the day, so I work full-time Monday to Friday,' she explained. 'I also coach at Blackburn Rovers Centre of Excellence two nights a week and have a game with them on Saturday mornings, and then Sheffield two nights a week, Tuesdays and Thursdays, and then a game on a Saturday or Sunday or whenever they're on. It's a pretty hectic week – football every night, whether it's at Blackburn or Sheffield. That's something I'll have to look over and review.'

After her first few games in charge of a WSL side, she was still settling into the role, but she was clear about her coaching ethos and why her players had bought into it.

'It's always been the same, really – how I've always worked is that we want to be a possession football team, play attractive football, because that's what Sheffield FC is about. It always has been under Helen. Then as soon as we lose possession the girls have to show 100 per cent aggressive attitude, pressing football, win the ball back, work hard. Yesterday they really bought into that away at Bristol, 0-0 at half-time and we had to make two subs within 30 minutes. I said to the girls at half-time, "One hundred and ten per cent – you graft and you graft, you do that and we'll get a result," and they bought into that. They've instantly gone out there, worked hard for each other and the club, and got a point against what we would expect to be the league winners this year.

'Something that's going to be new to them this year, and I think that's why we struggled a little bit against Durham [in their first match of the WSL season], they're used to winning games, they're used to them going there, being the big dogs, battering teams. That's not going to happen now, they're the ones that are going to be getting battered, but I think they're slowly realising that they go in as underdogs, they've got to graft, and they've done that, they've done exactly what we've asked of them.'

Sheffield's development team also showed those qualities, taking a 2-0 lead and then stumbling to 2-2 before reasserting themselves in the closing stages to secure a 4-2 win.

Mitchell, now officially a part-time member of Sheffield club staff as general manager, had been spending some time in recent weeks coaching the development team, following Johnson's appointment with the first team.

'We've now appointed someone, so that's a big weight off me, because doing two training sessions a week and a matchday on a Sunday has been killing me, as well as everything else I'm supposed to be doing!' she admitted. 'I'm hoping after another month things will settle in and I'll be doing what I'm meant to be doing and not an awful lot else, but yes, it's been frantically busy since Christmas. I feel like I need to sleep for about three days.'

After spending so many years running the club single-handedly, Mitchell was finding it tough to compartmentalise and focus on her new role.

'The trouble is, when you've been doing it voluntarily and you've been fitting it into evenings and weekends, you keep doing that,' she explained. 'You're also now doing two and a half days a week plus a weekend, but you find you do nothing else apart from go to work and then football. I do feel like I've been doing that for about ten months, so things need to settle down a bit. You can't do everything, and we have to get more people involved. We always said the first year was going to be a big learning curve for us and we will make changes along the way, but with every week that passes, we are refining things and putting things right. Hopefully by August time we'll be on a bit more of an even keel – I hope so, anyway! If the results are good, everything looks a lot happier and getting out of bed is a lot easier!'

Sheffield's first home fixture in the WSL had taken place a few days before, and Mitchell was still recovering from the experience, describing it as exhausting as well as a step into the complete unknown.

'We're used to crowds, on a good day, of 150, and we know what that looks like and we can manage it,' she explained. 'We know that; we've got the experience of having dealt with that. We didn't know how many we were going to get – we had a rough idea that we were going to get about 500, just because of the people who'd told us they were coming, but we don't know what that looks like, we're not used to that. How does that impact on car parking? How does that impact on turnstiles? How does that impact on the snack bar?

'We learnt an awful lot and I went away a bit deflated, but that's me – I concentrate really on the things that need to be put right rather than the things that went pretty well on the night. Generally the feedback was really good, everybody seemed to have a positive experience, lots of people tweeting, lots of people e-mailing, texting me saying what a fantastic night it was.

'All in all, it's a big learning curve for us, that was a good marker, and we did enough well enough, but there are things that we need to address to do better for the next one.'

One of the biggest changes for the club was the increased budget required to run a WSL team – and the extra staffing required.

'Personnel equals money. We've gone from a volunteer workforce to a paid workforce – and it's the scale of it as well,' said Mitchell. 'From me doing an awful lot, plus a few coaches, it's gone to me plus six or seven other behind the scenes staff and up to ten coaching and support staff, with strength and conditioning and doctors and physios, so it's a way, way bigger organisation.

'There's a very small number of clubs at the top level that have the resources to do it properly, and then a lot of other clubs that are actually struggling. There's a real danger that things could run away from the league if they're not careful, and they'll end up with a very uncompetitive league with three teams at the top winning everything and everyone else wondering why on earth they're putting the money in, because it's not insignificant money, when they've got absolutely no chance of winning everything.'

Sheffield were a special case as well – from the two divisions of the WSL, they were one of only two teams not attached to a professional men's club. Mitchell was worried that women's football might end up as a carbon copy of the men's game, reliant on money, and requiring handouts and running up debt in order to operate at the highest level.

'Just from our own experience jumping up from the Prem, it has been really hard. We're a non-league club, and I don't know that there'll be any other club that does that, I really can't see it, to be honest. I think all the clubs that are likely to be part of it are attached to Football League clubs, this year or in the future. Brighton, Charlton, they've got good support from their men's club already. They're going to need that.

'I've spoken to managers of [Women's] Premier League clubs – they've rung me to say, "How have you done it, how has it stacked up, what sort of finances are we looking at really?" When I've told them what we're running at, they're like, "We had no idea," because the figures in front of them are already two years out of date – what they're actually running at is an awful lot more. Even when we put the bid in, there were averages that we were working to, and within a year things have moved on so much from there. You wonder where within a year it's going to end up if things aren't put in place to rein it in a bit.'

Sheffield's only full-time member of staff was Richard Tims, the club chairman, working across all the teams. When his involvement with the club started, the men were playing at the famous old Don Valley athletics stadium – a well-loved venue, perhaps, but hardly suitable for football. A printer by trade, he used his experience in business and interest in marketing to create a new strategy for the club's growth. He was the man who met with Mitchell back in 2003 and brought the women's team into the fold.

'Helen now has driven Sheffield FC from the very bottom of women's football to almost the top on what we call in our marketing and resource strategy "air and goodwill",' he said. 'She's done an absolutely amazing job single-mindedly.'

Part of Tims's plans for the future was to develop a ground for the club somewhere closer to the city centre – somewhere with facilities, somewhere they could call home, and somewhere suitable for the club's historic standing. After all, Sheffield FC are the world's first football club – the place where the laws of the game were first written down. Although they might get overlooked a touch in England, what with their big city rivals Wednesday and United, globally the Sheffield FC brand has an impact – and Tims gives credit to ex-Barcelona president Joan Laporta for inspiring his marketing strategy.

'The FA put me together with the Catalan Football Federation in 2003,' Tims explained, 'and I ended up chatting to him, and he invited me to the stadium the next day. I thought I was just going on the museum tour, but he met me on the steps, out of season, 9.30 in the morning, and showed me the inner workings of Barcelona football club.

'What I learned on that trip was all the people in that organisation were more amazed to meet me than I was to meet them.

'That's when the penny dropped. Why are people in Sheffield not amazed at what they've got on their own door-step? Why is the UK obsessed by the Premier League? So I started a marketing campaign to let the world know where football kicked off.'

Tims's efforts paid dividends, with the club picking up the FIFA Order of Merit in 2004 alongside Real Madrid.

'You've got the biggest and richest football club in the world, and then you've got little grassroots Sheffield FC. You share the same award and honour, and that's fantastic as a marketeer. Whether you support Real Madrid or Sheffield, we all love the game. From a business perspective, if you're the first football club in the world, does every football club in the world not genetically come from you? Should they not love you?'

That worldwide significance was at the forefront of Tims's mind as he worked to secure the club a local base.

'We've been gifted a piece of land by the city council on the very first field that Sheffield FC played on and where the rulebook was written, so we have a project called the Home of Football to relocate the first football club back home,' he explained.

'If we had somewhere we could call our own, just on a training level, we'd just be able to do so much more with it. That's what we're working towards,' said Mitchell. 'It's not like we can go to the men's club and say we need £3m to be able to do this, because we haven't got it. Some have, but not many have.'

Tims acknowledged that Mitchell and her team were in a difficult position – of the 19 WSL clubs in 2016, only Sheffield and Durham were not attached to a professional men's club, meaning that there was no subsidy coming their way from that affluent source.

'Certainly in WSL1 the gap's massive,' said Tims. 'Building the Home of Football could become a pilgrimage for all football fans to visit where it started. You can then merchandise membership. That's always been a plan of mine for the last ten years, really, as England were bidding for the 2018 World Cup. I thought if England were successful in winning that bid, would every football fan not want to visit where it all started?'

While the men's team at Sheffield will likely always stay at a non-league level, the women made the step up to semi-professionalisation, meaning the club had to entirely reassess their budget for 2016.

'For us it's been a massive shock in terms of our resource,' admitted Tims. 'That's a massive jump. I think looking at what the WSL are doing, that's helped. They have a structure that you are meant to follow, so it does give you those guidelines that you don't get in men's football, so sitting down and working out a marketing plan is, I think, to our advantage, but yes, it's going to be an interesting first season. It is a massive leap for us – we are the first team to get there on merit. If I was an accountant at the start of this journey, I'd say Sheffield FC competing next year against Man City and Arsenal is a ridiculous story. But we're ambitious, we're entrepreneurial, and we're going to give it our best shot. I think the challenges off the field are more than they are on it.'

Fortunately, those within the club were now all very supportive of the women's team – despite the misgivings they might have had at the start due to preconceptions and lingering prejudice.

'We were led by a committee for 150 years,' said Tims, referring to the sense of tradition in the club, 'but actually, you know what, those people now have completely embraced it [the women's team]. Some of the guys who have been there for 50 years now absolutely love it, like our president. It was the right thing to do. That's proving the point now.'

As Mitchell had noted earlier in the season, Tims had always been optimistic about Sheffield's chances of reaching the upper echelons of the women's game; but he happily agreed that a similar journey would never be possible for the men's first team. Still, he pointed out, success and financial glory were not the reasons for the club's existence.

'We're not trying to be Man Utd, Man City or Real Madrid,' he said. 'We just want to be the ultimate grassroots football club – integrity, respect and community, remembering where the game came from. It's not all about money. We're proving that. We can compete in women's football – I doubt we'll be able to do that in men's football.

'We've missed the boat. People ask me why Sheffield United and Sheffield Wednesday are more famous than us. The two gentlemen who wrote the laws of the game did it for the love of the game – not for money. We want to remain as close to those principles as possible – I think that's refreshing. If you can be that social conscience to tell youngsters coming through that 99.9 per cent of people around the world don't play football for money, they play for different reasons, that's what our club represents.'

※ ※ ※ ※ ※

It was Lisa Giampalma who scored the goal to secure Sheffield's place in the Women's Super League.

In stoppage time of their play-off match against WPL southern champions Portsmouth, she picked up the pass from Jodie Michalska, and rounded young goalkeeper Courtney Trodd to slot home and seal promotion.

'I remember Jodie passing it to me and I just remember thinking, "I'm going to score," which I'm not normally like, I'm not very confident at all,' she recalled. 'I just remember thinking, "I have to score," and I remember thinking what I was going to do when [Trodd] was coming out, and just scoring – going crazy.'

Giampalma and Michalska are good friends off the pitch, having played together for many years.

'I was looking for her all the time and set her up for a lot of goals. It was nice for it to be the other way round in that match, with me the longest-serving player,' said Giampalma.

Her memories of the game were very clear, not clouded by the excitement of the goal or winning the ultimate prize of promotion.

'I remember quite a lot of it, I think. Obviously I remember it being a very good game and it being very competitive. It could have gone either way, Claire [Wallhead, the Sheffield goalkeeper] made some amazing saves. That topped it off, it couldn't have gone any better for me personally or the team. It was absolutely amazing scoring that.'

Giampalma had joined Sheffield in 2007, moving there after finishing university in Loughborough, and playing an integral role in the club's development.

'When I first went there, the first training session was on a park,' she said with heavy irony, adding that the facilities and the standard of football she had been used to at Loughborough were much better. Yet she had broken her leg in her final season at university, and needed to get back to full fitness; training and playing with Sheffield would be able to help her with that. 'I was thinking, "What am I doing, really?" but I did really enjoy the people, and the set-up was actually very good in terms of the coaching and things.

'Gradually the next few months we got really good facilities and everything was very professional; even back then, when we were playing at a really low level, everything was very professional, and it has been all the way through in terms of good coaching, good ways of doing things. If you don't train you don't play – so many good players, at a lot of clubs, get preferential treatment. It wasn't like that at all, we were all equal, and properly so. That's why I stayed.'

As Sheffield under Helen Mitchell's leadership developed, new and better players were added to the squad, but with the core players remaining.

'We've always had such a good team spirit and Mitch has been very good about bringing in the right players at the right time,' said Giampalma. 'She's never brought in loads of players and got rid of loads, it's always been a gradual process of people choosing to leave when they felt they couldn't play at that level any more, as we went up quite quickly – but it was always on very good terms. We got new players in positions where we needed them rather than [adding] anyone that was good, and the right people that would fit with the group. That was really important for us to do so well.'

In her near-decade with the club, she was involved with every single trophy they won, making over 270 appearances and scoring more than a century of goals. Yet she announced her retirement before the WSL season even began. The changes at the club had shaken her, and she re-evaluated what she wanted from her life and leisure time.

'It changed a lot. Obviously I've been there for a long time and it's been very consistent in how it's been and how we've done things, and then the new manager came in – who has since gone,' she explained. 'It was very different, and I didn't really enjoy it. That was the main thing. During last season I was thinking I was going to stop at the end of the season because I wanted to do other things, like running and stuff – that's also a big reason as well. When we got into the Super League I decided to give it a go and carry on, but then I trained for a few months and just wasn't enjoying it, really.'

When she decided to hang up her boots, the tributes were fulsome. The club's official statement quoted Giampalma as saying, 'It's been a really difficult decision, and I'm very sad to leave the club as it's been such a huge part of my life for so long, but I feel the time is right and I wish both the development and first team players all the best in their WSL venture.'

It also quoted Mitchell as praising Giampalma with the words, 'It's an incredible story – one you couldn't write. Lisa scored the goal which won us our first ever trophy in a 1-1 draw against Keighley on the final day of the season [in 2008 for the region's Division One South league title], and scored the goal which secured our most recent title – seven years later in the FA WPL Championship play-off final. Lisa's announcement last week has been tough news to take for the current players, but I think everyone also appreciates the timing and respects what has obviously been a very emotional and hard decision for Lisa to take.

'She will always be valued and respected here, and it will be very difficult for anyone to replicate what she's achieved or to break her record of all-time appearances for the club. On behalf of everyone, I'd like to thank Lisa for her unfailing loyalty, her unparalleled contribution to the progress the club has made, and for her humility, selflessness and sheer hard work.'

Indeed, Giampalma was still keen on sheer endeavour and hard grind – with her evenings and weekends suddenly free, she trained for and then ran the Paris marathon in March 2016, but her thoughts were always with the club, hoping that the squad would settle now that Zoe Johnson was in post with Mitchell's support.

'She's ridiculously dedicated. She's dedicated her life to this club over the past 12 years. People see that and it rubs off on them. People want to play for Mitch and they then put in the extra bit of effort. People have put football first – things like booking holidays because of football people have not done even in the early lower leagues. We've not missed key players at key times. That comes through Mitch's dedication and commitment. They see her not missing anything. We are all in it together.'

Giampalma expected that Johnson would develop into a great coach and manager, learning plenty from her more experienced colleague.

'She is also very committed – she lives miles away, she's here every session, every match obviously, she doesn't miss anything,' she said. 'She does have a good relationship particularly with the younger players because she's been the manager of the development team and she's keen to bring them through, but with the older players, I think she's got good relationships. I think when she first came, it wasn't quite like that, but she has shown what she's like and what she can do, and people have obviously respected her for that.

'Now she has the respect of the players, of the team, and she's done well. I think she has grown up a bit; obviously she is young – when she first came maybe she was a little bit naïve, but I think she's really good now and she'll do a good job, especially with the people around her, like Mitch, who have got the experience, and I think they are working really well together now, so that's good.'

Giampalma left her boots firmly at home, but she still went to watch Sheffield's first game in the WSL, which she found a difficult experience.

'The first game was very hard for me not to be involved, but obviously I went and watched, but it was horrible!' she admitted. 'Especially because a lot of old players were playing still, and I felt like…'

She stopped, and thought about it.

'I don't have a great deal of confidence, and I'm always questioning whether I'm good enough, and have done that for the past few years, really. But…'

She stopped again, clearly considering whether her next words would be taken as they were meant.

'I feel that I probably am, maybe, so it was hard to not be involved, thinking maybe I could have been. I will still be involved, still go to watch – and maybe a bit more.'

A bit more?

'I have actually since been back to training in the last few weeks. We'll see what happens.'

Would she consider coming out of retirement and giving WSL football a go after all?

'I don't know,' she said, clearly slightly uncomfortable with the question. 'It depends whether they want me, which I haven't had a conversation about yet. Obviously they've brought in quite a few players and things, but I think I would sign, yes, if they wanted me. I don't know. It's early days. At the moment I'm just trying to get into enjoying it, because I wasn't enjoying it at all, and I didn't want to get into the situation where I hated football and hated the club. I'm getting to the point now where I'm enjoying it – really enjoying being around everyone again. I'm going to see what happens, really.'

※ ※ ※ ※ ※

Eastlands, more commonly known and referred to as the Etihad Stadium, towers over the city skyline. Even the garish, gigantic supermarket opposite comes nowhere near its size. This area of Manchester was regenerated for the 2002 Commonwealth Games, hence the athletics track, the indoor arena, and the velopark which gives the nearby tram station its name. The main stadium itself, once the City of Manchester Stadium, became the home of Manchester City, and rebranded in name and décor accordingly.

Across the road, connected by a sweeping white footbridge, is the Academy Stadium, home of the men's junior sides, and of Manchester City Women. A 7,000-capacity ground, with two all-seated stands and a terrace behind each goal, a hospitality lounge for players and guests, a press box with plug sockets and wifi, this is a perfect football ground in miniature.

Next to the stadium, taking up a sizeable proportion of the 88-acre complex, are the training facilities, for which Manchester City have become increasingly famous – not just because what they offer is state-of-the-art, but because their women train alongside the men and junior sides, with equal access to everything – the gym, the pitches – and their own recreational space too.

The ethos is that Manchester City is one club, and thus all of its players contribute to that and have the same support structures. The physiotherapists work with all the squads; the communications team manage publicity and content for all the squad; and so on.

Of course, there are some elements of each team that are unique, and part of that is their marketing. Women's football in England has been firmly marketed to girls and young women since the launch of the Women's Super League.

Manchester City, as a club without a strong history of women's football before their leap up into the WSL, had been considering more carefully than some others exactly how they should be advertising to potential fans in order to boost attendances.

'When we broke up for the mid-season break last year for the World Cup, we did a review, as we do every year, we review how the first part of the season went, and even though attendances have been okay, relatively good, compared to what you normally get at women's football, I was keen to look into why we weren't getting more people through the door, particularly our men's team's fans,' explained Gavin Makel, the club's head of women's football.

'It just suddenly dawned on me, really, that people may be not coming because they don't feel any affinity towards the team, any connection. We all grow up supporting a club at a young age; I'm from Newcastle, they were my team growing up – I'm fully Manchester City now, obviously – but we all have our own team and it's not a case of just being able to say, "We're Manchester City, slap the badge on it, you've got to go and support them," you've got to buy into it.'

To encourage this emotional tie to the women's team and its players, the club launched a campaign under the slogan 'Dreams Start Here', with Izzy Christiansen the focus of the first poster.

'It was basically her holding a trophy she won when she was 11 playing in a girls' tournament, and then they had the shadow of her holding the Conti Cup trophy, when she scored the winning goal – and then it says "Dreams start here",' said Makel. The club also used a video clip of Christiansen's brother, talking about his memories of them playing football together as children, and his pride in her achievements since then. They followed that up with a similar poster featuring Daphne Corboz – an image of her playing as a six-year-old alongside an image of her playing now – and footage of her father.

'Her parents live in New Jersey, and he said, "She's my daughter, please look after her, it's the first time she's lived away out of the country, she doesn't know anyone"' – just again to get people to feel, "Ah right, if that was my daughter, then I'd want someone else to support her."'

The club were considering how to extend the campaign in the future, and whether it would have a similar impact on the

general public as well as City fans. It had certainly changed
the demographic attending City women's games, with the
most recent attendee profile indicating that a significant
proportion of fans were girls under 16 coming along with
older male relations, whether that was their dad, uncle or
grandfather.

'We didn't really see that correlation before we started
the campaign,' emphasised Makel. 'We need to ramp it up a
little bit more and look at different ways of how to execute it.'

Makel and his team at City were clearly ambitious for the
club, on and off the pitch.

'It's this season where you'll really see the impact of the
World Cup – if people are still engaged with it,' he said.
'There's definite challenges, but we had a good crowd here
on Wednesday [for the first WSL game of the season], and
we had a good crowd here when we played Rosengard as well
[in a pre-season friendly], we had over 1,000 for that game.
Our average was 1,500 last year, which was the highest in the
league, and if we can get that anywhere over 2,000 average,
I'll be really happy about that. The fact we haven't got any
major women's tournaments [in the summer of 2016] – yes,
it's nice to be able to bounce off the back of that, but we can
really focus as a league; as a group of clubs, we can really focus
on pushing the league a bit more, really. So hopefully we'll
get a good attendance today, although,' he glanced towards
the window, 'with Manchester weather elements, you never
know what that's going to do.'

% *%* *%* *%* *%*

Manchester City and Arsenal had begun their WSL seasons
with a win, and with both likely to be at the top end of the table
come the autumn this was inevitably going to be a fiercely
contested affair. Even the bank holiday goodwill could not
affect the aggressive, charged atmosphere, and the bitingly

cold wind could not chill the heat, with the partisan home crowd of almost 2,000 and fired-up home players feeding off each other's emotions.

Steph Houghton – playing against her former club – was first to get her name in the referee Michael Salisbury's notebook for bringing down Asisat Oshoala; she was followed five minutes later by Arsenal's Jemma Rose, who got sent off for an apparent foul on Nikita Parris. Even with ten players, the visitors contained the attacking threat of City, with the experienced Casey Stoney and young goalkeeper Sari van Veenendaal the stand-outs.

After an hour, the defence crumbled, with Leah Williamson's stumble leading to a goal for the second game running; this time she was under pressure from the lively Toni Duggan, who put in a terrific cross for Scottish international Jane Ross to head home. It was Duggan who put the game beyond reach, too, powering an excellent penalty past van Veenendaal after Dominique Janssen was adjudged to have tripped Parris, although it did appear to be outside the box.

The Arsenal players were unsurprisingly disgruntled after the game, with some expressing the opinion that Rose and Houghton's early fouls were similar and should have been punished accordingly, and that Janssen had got the ball from Parris outside the penalty area, making it a corner rather than a spot-kick.

Midfielder Fara Williams praised the team's attitude, saying, 'We've got great character in this team – we're not going to be out there with just ten players and not fight.'

Their opponents, conversely, were thrilled to take all three points. 'For any spectator, for our coaches, for their coaches, for everyone in the league, they know we're dominating these games,' enthused striker Toni Duggan.

Manager Nick Cushing acknowledged that the awkward season scheduling made it difficult to maintain consistency at times.

'You start to put a four- or five-game run together and then you've got a four-week break, but I'm not one to complain about the schedule: it is what it is,' he said. 'If we waste energy complaining about something we can't change, it'll take our focus off improving and working hard, so just concentrate all our energy on what we can control and that'll give us the best chance of being successful.'

The Women's Champions League quarter-finals were imminent, and Cushing's side would be in the next season's competition – which would begin at the end of the WSL, another scheduling glitch with the domestic summer season. Although it was months away, it was already in his mind.

'You do think about it at times when you're off the pitch,' he admitted, 'but when you're on the training pitch or working at the gym or on a matchday, it's not in your immediate focus. I think it will start to become a focus later on in the year when the draw's made and we know who we're playing.

'We're not going to be seeded, we know that, it's our first year, so we could potentially get a really big draw, which is what we want really at this football club – top people, hard-working people, good players, let's put ourselves against the best and see where we're at. After it, win lose or draw, we'll review it and we'll go again.'

While some of the players made their way into the lounge to help themselves to a hot meal – chilli con carne, barbecue chicken and Mediterranean vegetables were all on offer, along with juices – other City stars stayed out in the cold for a bit longer.

The match was televised live, meaning some post-match media duties for Cushing and Duggan; but they also took the time to meet their young fans in the north-east corner of the stadium, the area reserved for this kind of meet-and-greet. Fans got the chance to talk to and take pictures with their favourites as well as grab a couple of autographs – indeed, the matchday programme gives away a photo postcard each game so that supporters can collect them all and get signatures if they want.

'You get a good day out here with the family and you get to feel part of the football club as well,' said Makel. 'Maybe it's a step as well for young children who get a little bit scared about going to a men's game because of all the people and the noise and stuff like that, but they can come here, and it's a different, friendly atmosphere.'

Though City's facilities were exceptional, everyone involved with the club took pains to point out that they were only a small part of their growth and success. Nick Cushing had been with the club in a variety of roles for eleven years, and had seen it develop and change hugely.

'I don't think another club can compete with the facilities here,' he said. 'But two things can happen with a facility like this, it's world-leading. You can come here and use all the resources and improve and use it all to be the best you can be, whether you're a staff member or a player; or you can come here, enjoy the luxury and take your foot off the gas and be complacent. As staff, we've got to push the players all the time and raise the expectations. We're in this magnificent stadium – do it justice by performing well, and at the moment we're doing that; we've not lost here since March [2015], 23 games unbeaten.'

'One thing that we always say is that facilities don't make players, it's about the people, and fortunately we've got some very good people at this football club in all departments,' reflected Makel. 'That's more key for us in terms of when we're recruiting players as well – are you the right person that's going to fit what we're about, what we do? The group of players we've got now are a great group of girls, who believe in what we're doing. When we talked to Steph [Houghton] originally, a few years ago now, this place was a scrapheap.

'There was mud everywhere. I remember taking her round in the Land Rover 4x4, hard hat, wellington boots on, and I was saying, "This is the stadium, your training pitch is going to be here." That was a great leap of faith for someone like Steph, and Jill [Scott] because at the time we hadn't played at this level and they'd obviously had great success. There were still a lot of people before we opened who disbelieved in us and the fact that we were going to be playing here. You want for nothing here and the only thing that's stopping you from developing as a player or as an employee is yourself, because you've got everything you could possibly want in terms of access to resources, or facilities, or expertise among staff.

'It's a great environment to work in, and that's been key in the design stage as well; a group of people went around the world looking at different sports facilities to see the best bits that we can put in place. It's a good recruitment tool, and I'd be lying if I said it wasn't, but I'd like to think that the reason why players come here is more than just bricks and mortar.'

*% *% *% *% *%

The young fans and those new to the game might not have noticed her, but in the lounge during the game was an England legend.

Sylvia Gore was part of the generation that played during the FA ban. She began playing in women's teams as a precocious pre-teen, encouraged by her supportive parents who would take her to matches on the bus and back. She worked tirelessly as an adult to create a structure for girls to play football at local level. She has picked up honours from UEFA, the FA and the UK government along the way, and accepted the role of Manchester City ambassador on International Women's Day in 2016.

City as a women's team was not in existence when Gore was playing, but she spent her career in the north-west for teams such as the famous Corinthians. When she was a teenager, she enjoyed going on continental tours with the club, prioritising that over almost everything else.

'When I was young, 16 or 17, and about to go on tour, I thought, "Shall I give up my job?" I was only filing then – you know, when you first get a job, you'd get a filing job in those days – and I thought, "I'm going to give it up," she recalled.

She chuckled, and reiterated, 'I gave my job up to go and play football abroad!'

She laughed more. 'I did that sort of thing. I never came unstuck. I always came out with a job at the end of the day.'

Were some employers more supportive than others when she was looking for time off to play, then? The laughter continued. 'If they didn't give me the time off I just left!'

Of course, in the 21st century, Gore acknowledged that was perhaps not quite such a viable plan of action for semi-professional female players, and she felt sympathy for them.

'Some of the [Women's] Premier League players struggle because their employers don't recognise [women's football], and they can't get time off because the fixtures now are in the midweek – that's the difficult part of it,' she said. 'It's all right if you're professional and you're being paid for it, like the ones at City are, and Arsenal, and Chelsea. When it comes to the Premier League, before you get to that stage, of the Super League, it's difficult for them. It's something that you're not going to get over unless the Premier League turns professional as well, which I can't see at the minute. It's a shame, really. I know some teachers, and a couple of them have packed in because their employer isn't giving them the time off.'

Even for the professional players, Gore was quick to think about what they might do in the future.

'They can either go into coaching jobs or stay involved with the club in some capacity and they get paid for it,' she said, and pointed out that many of the older players had been forward-thinking enough to take a university degree in preparation for their retirement. 'It's not like in the men's game when you play professional football and you get megabucks for it – you sign a contract and you come away with millions even if you don't finish your contract off and they get rid of you. We're not at that stage with the women's game and I don't think we'll be at that stage for a while yet.'

Gore praised the FA's investment, but hoped to see more money going into the grassroots game to develop the talent pipeline, and to avoid the dangers of relying on men's clubs to subsidise the women's game. As someone who had been involved with running the Women's FA without genuine support from the national governing body, she acknowledged how far women's football had progressed, but thought there was much still to do.

'We struggled trying to keep the teams going and get a league going because when they don't recognise it at the top level, you're in difficulties, aren't you?' she said. 'Don't get me wrong, it's progressed immensely. I only wish that I played in this era.'

A pang of envy at seeing the facilities on offer to the Manchester City women would perhaps be understandable – but Gore was happy for those players.

'I'm delighted to be their ambassador – not because they're successful but because the whole club is run in a professional way, men's, women's, juniors,' she said. 'Everything is spot-on. I can't fault it at all, I'm really honoured to be part of that.'

She felt honoured too to have been part of the long line of women who had worked so hard to get women's football recognised, enabling the new generation of players to get paid for their work, and giving future generations the dream of playing professionally.

'We needed to get it to a certain level, and we *have* got it to a certain level,' she said with satisfaction. 'I wouldn't swap my career for anyone or anything, because I earned a lot of honours, a lot of medals, a lot of trophies, and [we've been] recognised a lot in the last 40, 50 years.'

She talked about setting up girls' teams in Knowsley a few decades previously, recalling fondly the enthusiasm of the players but the reticence of some parents to support their daughters.

'The parents, they'd say, "Well, they're not going to get anything out of football, because they're girls." If they look back at it now they'd have [eaten] their words because they can now achieve and look forward to what they can do.'

So was there any small part of her that wished she was playing now rather than going through that half-century of struggles? Gore seemed slightly surprised by the question; this inveterate fighter clearly would not wish to revel in relative luxury rather than win any of her battles.

'I wouldn't swap it for the world, no!'

Up for the cups

CHILDREN ran around the playground as joggers ran through the park in Stepney. The nights were lengthening and the skies were clear, making it a perfect place to enjoy a brisk spring evening.

Casting one's eyes towards the park entrance, it was easy to notice the building work going on around the 3G pitches and the tall fences caging them. When Leyton Orient arrived for their training session, they had to walk the long way round as their usual door was locked.

Still, the floodlights were in place, beaming across the turf, illuminating a sizeable turnout for Orient's last practice before perhaps their biggest game of the season – the Mayor's Cup Final. They had accepted that their chances of promotion were limited after the winter weather played havoc with their fixtures and impacted on their consistency, but they could still grab some silverware in this local tournament.

The imminent big game had, unsurprisingly, encouraged attendance. Even captain Danni Griffiths, self-deprecating about the number of times she was late for training due to work commitments, was there right at the start. 'Last session of the season, and I'm finally here on time!' she grinned.

A few days earlier, she had explained just how she managed to juggle her football with her career.

'I'm a solicitor and I find it quite hard to get out of work in time for training sometimes,' she said. 'I qualified a year ago, so for the last year I've been a bit more in charge of my time, I can work late or work weekends instead, so it's been a lot better, but sometimes I do get pulled into a meeting by my boss at seven o'clock.'

Her squad evidently did not mind about her occasional lateness, responding to her calls of, 'Come on, girls,' encouraging them to speed up and listen to their coach. Part of her role as captain was to be a point of contact for the players, and act as a liaison between them and the coach.

'Some younger members of the team like to come and talk to me first before they go and ask Chris something or someone else something,' she said. 'Chris can't keep a handle on all of us all the time, so I make sure we're on the straight and narrow, working hard. Generally being bossy, I think everyone would describe me as, but that's fine!'

Danni grinned. She was obviously reasonably satisfied with the team's progress over the season, but was still ambitious for more.

'Last year we didn't have a consistent squad, so we did struggle a bit towards the end of the season,' she said, explaining that the lack of contention of trophies made it difficult to motivate some of the players to attend and play. 'This year is a lot better.

'At the start we had a few games where we struggled to score, struggled to finish, which cost us a few results, but since a few weeks before Christmas and after then we can't really complain. After then we've only lost to Fulham and Wimbledon, who are two of the better teams. We'll be in contention next year as well. We've shown that we can hold our own.'

Although she was only 26, Danni was a ten-year veteran having played for Colchester when she was just 16. She was pleased that Orient had affiliated with the men's club, having experienced the benefits of that when she was in the United first team.

'We feel much more part of a whole club,' she said. 'When I played for Colchester and we had that set-up, we were affiliated with the men's team, they publicised us, put our match reports in the programme, things like that. When you say you play for Leyton Orient it carries much more weight. Everyone recognises it and it means now we've got Leyton Orient fans coming along to games, asking for autographs, which is strange, very strange, and lots more interviews.'

Indeed, some Orient fans were asking whether they could buy replica kits of the women's team – because, yes, finally, they had their new kits, the same as the men's, but with their own sponsors – Fran Cagetti's company. They even had their own smart training gear in a bright orange colour, marked with their squad numbers. What was more, since they had started playing in the new kit, they had gone unbeaten.

'It looks really, really good, and I think it's boosted morale: for some reason we play better in a red kit as opposed to yellow or green,' said Danni.

She expected that Orient could operate at a higher level in years to come, but having already played in a higher league, she was well aware of some of the changes that would need to be made to ensure they could compete.

'In previous seasons we've beaten teams a couple of leagues above us. I think our squad is better now,' she said, but added that against some of the higher-ranked teams, in the latter stages of the game the difference in their fitness levels began to be obvious.

'We only have one training session a week. If you're not playing on a Sunday, which for most people is their match fitness, it's really, really hard. So I think that's something we'd need to look into if we were going any further up; we'd have to train more, or when we have postponements we'd have to have some kind of way of playing. We did five-a-side when one of our games was cancelled, we just arranged it ourselves, or arrange friendlies. Playing consistently together, which we've seen, when we're playing week in week out together, we are ten times better.'

Their consistency and team ethic were rewarded with the Mayor's Cup – an absolute rout for Leyton Orient, beating Tower Hamlets of the Greater Women's Football League Division One 6-0 to pick up the trophy. Oly Diamond had returned for the match, taking a place on the substitutes' bench, travelling down from Liverpool where she had taken a new role back in February and which had forced her to miss the previous three games. She had played in the first match with the new kit ('I don't think we realised quite how much it mattered until we'd got it,' she said) and had also received her new squad number along with it – 6, one of the three choices she had given Brayford as he attempted to make sure everyone got something they were happy with ('He puts up with a lot. He is really excellent,' Oly praised him).

'I thought they'd be a bit more of a challenge, especially physically,' said Oly, reflecting on their cup final. 'When we play teams lower than us, you never know; and even if the quality of football and individual players aren't overall as good, they can be very physical. Mentally I was preparing for quite a physical game, and sometimes the other team plays slower, that can really impact your game, so I was expecting to deal with those situations, but everyone was really up for it.

'We said we were worried that everyone's mentality was thinking about winning without playing, but yes, I think right off the bat everyone was really excited about the game. We just imposed our play on them instead of letting them get a look-in, really. I think that's also a combination of the last couple of games: we've played really, really well as a team, we were still training, so we were in the flow and on form.'

That was the last match of Orient's season and their final time together as an entire squad for the next two months.

'We'll come back for pre-season at the end of June, July, and start again,' explained Danni. 'We'll work on fitness, getting back into playing week in week out, we'll have a few friendlies against teams that are both below and above us in the league.'

She was not expecting Brayford to make too many changes to the core of the squad.

'I don't think there's desperate need – just add one or two who will add something to the squad,' she said. 'I think it's important that we stay as a group and build on what we've already got. We've had a lot of new players in who have now integrated, so it's now working with that squad.'

Brayford confirmed that he was planning to run some trial matches in the summer to identify potential new talent as well as work on bringing together a development team, the Orient players of the future.

'The big thing for us is to keep this group together,' he said. 'I hope this season we'll be able to play pre-season games with as big a chunk of the first team as available, and we'll try and set it up with teams from a higher division, hopefully WSL or WPL teams, and they can test themselves, against players who are quicker and stronger and technically very dangerous.

'In pre-season we need to get our goals aligned and make sure the team are a constant group, make sure we're focused on what we need to do to win the title and make sure that's reflected in everything – do the preparatory work, [ensure] we're as professional as we can be within the restrictions [we have] on and off the field. With respect to [league champions AFC] Wimbledon, they went off like a train and they got goals in the 88th, 89th minutes. That's a tribute, that's what you need as champions. We can certainly do the same.'

The road to Europe

THE New York Stadium is just over the road from Rotherham United's old home, Millmoor. The new ground, an out-of-town construction, with easy access to the roads, the bus terminal and the train station. Its Football League charter marks, highlighting the club's dedication to being family-friendly, are proudly displayed on the glass doors to the main stand.

In recent years, this has been one of the FA's favoured venues for staging internationals for teams other than the men's seniors. It was given the job in April 2016 of hosting England's Euro 2017 qualifier against Belgium, the Lionesses' first home game of the New Year. The FA has been historically keen to ensure that the women's internationals are played around the country, giving more local fans the chance to see the team.

Laudable, perhaps, but Rotherham's task was complicated, once again, by scheduling – the match was held on a Friday evening, creating problems for those fans who were committed enough to travel to the game on public transport, but found themselves struggling for a route back. Those with enough spare cash reserved themselves a hotel room; those with less money grabbed a seat on an overnight long-distance coach; and others simply decided that it was too much effort to go at all. Still, they were able to watch the match on television thanks to the BBC's renewed interest in broadcasting England's home games. More than that, it was on one of the Freeview channels – BBC Two, rather than on the red button or available solely online, as previous fixtures had been.

The FA was using this particular fixture to begin the build-up to the FA Cup Final in May, announcing a trophy tour and encouraging supporters to take a photo of themselves with it in the fan zone outside the ground. There was plenty else to see as well, with Rotherham's community department taking the opportunity to set up a goalscoring competition, inviting contestants to strike the ball through one of several holes in a giant red inflatable tent.

One little girl, aged about eight, was tenacious as she struggled to get to grips with the small ball and the technique necessary to guide it through the inflated walls. Finally she succeeded, and wheeled away, high-fiving the club staff, and shouting to her onlooking mother, 'I did it!'

Activities and an ever-expanding fan zone are key to the FA's plans to create a sense of occasion at big matches. There was also a dedicated girls' football zone, emblazoned with FA and Continental Tyres branding, and with a sound system blasting out recent chart hits, mostly by female vocalists. Teenage girls began to head towards the ground in pairs, many sporting the kits or training tops of their own favourite teams; families with small children made sure they were by the turnstiles in good time, striding past the stalls on the streets outside selling unofficial merchandise and the food vans boasting an enticing aroma of pork and onions.

When the gates opened at 6.30pm, the coaching staff of both sides were already setting out the cones and footballs for their training drills.

A trio of England players who missed out on the starting line-up and the bench were huddled by the side of the pitch, chatting to their media officer; coach Mark Sampson, in his formal FA suit but without a tie, took a slower walk across the turf.

Plenty of supporters had opted to invest in some of the goodies from the merchandise stands, with groups of siblings proudly sporting their half-and-half scarves, and irritating their neighbours with a quick blast of the air horns; two small girls proudly wore their replica shirts and had hair ribbons in England's colours of red, white and blue. Squads of girls from local clubs trooped in, excited and talkative; and large groups of teenage boys also took their seats in the stands.

Among the England fans there was also an impressive scattering of visitors cheering on Belgium's Red Flames, wrapped in flags, resplendent in black, yellow and red, and donning the customary comedy hats. What they made of the England mascots – a lion and a lioness in full kit – can only be imagined, but the home fans happily hugged the pair and posed for photographs, as did the players as they ran out to warm up. Fran Kirby, not even named on the substitutes' bench, spent some time before the match kicking a ball around with the two little girls who would be accompanying the team on to the pitch as mascots.

After the national anthems, the players and crowd joined in a minute's silence to remember the victims of terrorism around the world, but particularly those killed in an attack on Brussels Airport the previous month. The volume was boosted as soon as the referee blew her whistle as a duel between bands at opposite ends of the ground broke out; the England musicians immediately got a sing-song going with the theme from *The Great Escape*.

When goalkeeper Karen Bardsley missed her kick and allowed Janice Cayman's shot to crawl over the line, Sampson became increasingly infuriated, taking his frustrations out on the referee, striding out of his technical area and clapping his hands at her after a foul on Alex Scott. The poor fare served up by the home side was so un-enthralling that a Mexican wave broke out midway through the first half – always a sign of lack of engagement.

Half-time was much brighter as two young sides took to the pitch to play the final of the local girls' six-a-side tournament held in honour of the This Girl Can sports participation campaign. Both teams were clearly enjoying the opportunity to play on such a stage and in front of a decent crowd, and they were well rewarded with applause from the onlookers.

For England, however, the second half was not much brighter. Sampson lost his temper at the referee once more when the clock was stopped due to an injury to one of the assistant referees, tapping his watch frantically.

He was relieved to see his team equalise seven minutes from time, makeshift striker Jill Scott scrambling the ball home to send almost all of the 10,550 fans into a combination of ecstasy and sheer relief.

'I think the group of girls that we have would definitely feel that it's two points lost, but then it could have been worse, I suppose,' speculated the goalscorer after the match.

Scott pointed to the strength of England's defence, but admitted that goals were a little harder to come by.

'When Mark came in he made us tough to beat, defensively very tough to beat, and you can definitely see in our game that we're tough to beat. It takes time. We're creating chances, getting goals will be our next step now, we are working towards it, but change isn't something that happens overnight.'

She admitted there was something of a target on England's back, but argued this was a positive thing which highlighted the team's progress in recent months to a position as one of the countries to beat.

'I'd rather be doing well and teams wanting to beat you than being the other way round, which we were for a lot of years. It is added pressure for winners and winning teams, but you have to deal with that pressure.'

Karen Carney had brightened the game up when she came on as a second-half substitute. She had performed a similar role during the Women's World Cup, and many wondered why she had not been given the opportunity to stake a claim for a starting spot. Carney was clearly wary about being asked about this in case it could be misconstrued as disrespectful to either Sampson or her team-mates.

'I want to play football, I'm a really simple person,' she said. 'If I'm in the team, then fantastic, but if I'm not I'll always respect my manager because I believe he's making the best decision for England.'

Carney was just settling in at Chelsea following her close-season move from Birmingham, and her short time at the champions had already restored her love for football and her taste for winning, meaning that she was unhappy with a draw at home against Belgium.

'I like to win football matches,' she said. 'So I'm just frustrated today, I wanted England to win in front of a big crowd and on TV, but we'll compliment Belgium – sometimes when they put everything behind the ball it's really difficult to break down.'

She was already looking forward to the next match – away against Bosnia a few days later.

'I only look in the present. I'm focused on the next game. I just want to concentrate on Bosnia. If I'm part of it, great, if I'm not, I'll be a good team-mate and hope that we win.'

She got her chance – named from the start, and scoring the only goal of the game four minutes from time to secure England a much-needed three points, keeping them second in Group Seven.

%% %% %% %% %%

With England's away qualifiers rarely televised, fans were reliant on official accounts of the matches or on the social media updates of the incredibly dedicated fans who took the time to travel across the continent to watch.

'I got into women's football during the World Cup,' said England fan Sophie. She started going to WSL fixtures because of the cheapness of the tickets, and living in the Greater London area found that sometimes she could even manage two games in a day for just £10. She was one of the England fans who had booked themselves on to a coach to Rotherham and back for a minimal fee at a very inconvenient hour so they could cheer on the team.

'I went to my first England game last year, the Germany friendly [in Duisburg, a 0-0 draw in November 2015],' she recalled. 'I'd never been to Germany before, don't speak German, never been to an England game before, didn't know what to expect. I ran into some of the faithful England fans, and they took me under their wing. It made the experience a lot better, so I thought, "Let's do some more England games."'

'I went to the Bristol game straight afterwards as well [the Euro 2017 qualifier between England and Bosnia] – when you choose to sit in the front row and you realise you're not covered,' she rolled her eyes and tugged at her sleeve. 'I think this jacket's still wet. Everything about that – it was more of a hassle to get to Ashton Gate than to get to Germany.'

She could not go to the game in Bosnia due to a shortage of cash, but had already planned her next domestic trips, aiming to see every WSL team at home and to get in 60 matches before the season finished. It meant some long days – and when relying on public transport, some hefty cab fares to provide connections from stations to inaccessible grounds. She was understanding, though, and prepared to make those sacrifices.

'They go where they can get a pitch. If you can only get that patch of land, that's your home ground. Then you've got to negotiate when you can play there because obviously you've got other teams that play there, and that can't clash.'

A long-time fan of men's football, she was enthusiastic about the brand of the game played in the women's league.

'I'd rather see women play than men because men will dive, they're rolling around, they'll argue with the ref. Women enjoy playing football. There's the hard luck stories and all the shit they've had to put up with that was commonplace, and still is in some places: working two jobs, travelling ridiculous hours to get to training, and doing it so you can go out and play because you love playing. You don't get that so much in the men's game – it's the ego and it's the money.

'I watch a lot of men's football. I just watch a lot of football. But it gets so tiresome when players go down at the drop of a hat, they're arguing with the ref. I'm seeing that more in the women's game, unfortunately. It's almost like the motivation is different. I enjoy it.'

Fan fervour

I T usually takes little to create a social media storm, and changing a football match's kick-off time by an hour and 45 minutes would appear to be a relatively innocuous decision, on the face of it.

Arsenal Ladies' announcement that their derby against champions Chelsea on Thursday 21 April would be switched to 6pm, however, triggered all kinds of outrage.

Fans of women's football in England are used to seemingly illogical kick-off times. Arsenal's Champions League matches in previous seasons had been scheduled for midweek afternoons, hamstrung by Boreham Wood's home fixtures as well as their own domestic calendar.

This one, however, was a little different. Arsenal's reasoning for changing the kick-off time was the fact that the men's team were playing West Brom at the Emirates Stadium at 7.45pm. If the women's match was played earlier, it would give any interested parties the chance to watch the game live on television.

It also meant that a lot of people who were intending to head to Meadow Park after they finished work would now not make it in time for the game, hitting the attendance for what could prove to be a crucial game in deciding the destination of the WSL title.

Some were understanding, pointing out the difficulties with access to a ground not owned by the club, restricting the days on which it could be used.

Others were less so, pointing out that once again the women's game was at the mercy of the men, with a fixture being moved solely to enable potential TV viewers. Yes, they said, it may be that it was tricky to find a decent slot in the ground hire schedule that didn't clash with a men's game, and to fit in with BT Sport's intentions to broadcast WSL fixtures – but if that was the case, surely it would be simpler all round to take away some of the WSL complexity, restricting the season to the summer months rather than elongating it and ensuring a clash with the men's season, and sticking to Sunday afternoon kick-off times.

'They're not going to get good numbers,' predicted one fan.

The clubs stayed unsurprisingly but diplomatically silent on the entire subject.

Kelly Simmons of the FA was happy to give her views after the event, however, pointing out that the television viewing figures had been good, and parents had enjoyed being able to take their children to the match without delaying their bedtime too much.

'I think it's the biggest challenge the league's got, fixture scheduling,' she said. 'Numerous thousands watched that game who wouldn't have watched it, and that's what you've got to balance out – you don't want to upset the local fans either so it's a difficult decision every time.

'When I talked to [general manager] Clare Wheatley at Arsenal afterwards, she did have some great feedback from parents with young children who wouldn't have come to the game because it was too late to take the children home to bed on a school night, so it worked for them – but obviously it didn't work for those supporters who needed to get round the M25 after work. Ultimately down the road we desperately want to find a regular set TV slot that works for the women's game in conjunction with BT Sport – that's the aim, obviously.'

% *%* *%* *%* *%*

An hour before kick-off, scores of boys and their parents were milling around The Hive. It looked as if London Bees could expect a sizeable crowd for their WSL2 fixture against Bristol City Women.

On closer inspection, the crowds were there after a boys' academy session earlier in the day. Though the bar was filled – with plenty of people getting themselves a filling lunch plus a decent cup of coffee – many of them were not intending to stay for the women's match.

The Bees made their home at The Hive, the ground adopted by Barnet when they moved out of the famous old Underhill Stadium. It had been initially intended for Wealdstone, but financial problems meant the site was put up for tender, and Barnet moved in, first with training pitches and a centre of excellence there, then signing a ten-year lease in June 2015. Officially The Hive was intended as a temporary home for the club, and was never meant to be used for Football League matches; now, though, that condition has been navigated, and it is the long-term residence of the club.

Although it is in the London borough of Barnet, it is a fair way from High Barnet – it is just off Burnt Oak Broadway, the name for this section of the A5. The club had wanted to stay in their catchment area, and after their redevelopment plans for Underhill were quashed they had hoped to move to Barnet Copthall – but that plan was blocked, and the space was taken over by Saracens.

The Hive is a little oasis of football embedded into the community in its most literal sense. Where many clubs have moved out of residential areas to giant stadia with easy motorway access, The Hive, with its capacity a touch over 5,000, was constructed in space that was once used to build and house aircraft, became a playing field, and is still surrounded by houses. Behind the main stand runs the Jubilee line, part of the London Underground network. In this part of north-west London there is no need to hide it below street level, and instead it chugs backwards and forwards on its lengthy journey between Hertfordshire and the Olympic Park in Stratford.

The stadium campus also still boasts those training pitches used by the juniors – with a sign pinned to the outside of the fencing pointing parents to one particular area if they want to watch their offspring play. There are conferencing facilities too, and a screen on the street outside brightly advertises its offerings, from weddings to formal meetings. On this chilly afternoon, there were even programmes on sale, a new development in conjunction with a local university.

Inside the ground, the two teams were going through their stretches and warm-up routines, almost oblivious to whether or not they would have any spectators. Visitors Bristol City had been through a tumultuous 18 months. After Mark Sampson departed to take up the England manager's job, Willie Kirk had eventually taken over as head coach of the then Bristol Academy. The club were relegated from WSL1 at the end of 2015, and had promptly changed their name, aligning with Bristol City men's team; perhaps oddly the women had started their life aligned to their city rivals Bristol Rovers.

Still, the Bees had had barely an easier time of it; but David Edmondson had at least had some time by this point to make the squad his own. Indeed, it was a very different set of players than the ones who had finished the 2015 season – and a very different performance on the field. The Bees players looked well organised and confident – and equally as professional as their Bristol counterparts, a surprise, perhaps, bearing in mind their continuing semi-professional status, limiting their training to a handful of hours a week, in the evening after their day jobs or study commitments.

Yet it was that professionalism, that incision, that extra spark which made the difference as City put three goals past the Bees to make the scoreline much more flattering towards them than they really deserved.

'The girls are gutted, because it wasn't a three-goal difference,' said goalkeeper Sophie Harris. 'I do think it's a mental thing – the girls dropped their heads when we went one down, and we shouldn't – we need to pick ourselves up and find that equaliser. We've shown in the past few games that we can play football – we need to show that we want to win.'

The Bristol City captain Grace McCatty agreed that Bees could have acquitted themselves better, saying, 'They could have got a few goals themselves. It's hard when you get relegated – you don't really know what to expect from the teams, we don't really know how they play. They're a very physically fit team. Perhaps they surprised us but that's not to say we underestimated them.'

Part-time players in a league moving towards full professionalisation will always struggle and in England in 2016, even when women's teams are integrated into men's clubs, they tend to be a little way down the priority list. Yet even playing semi-professionally was something that could not be dreamt of by a previous generation of players. The London Bees have acknowledged a couple of key clubs that have fed into their establishment – one District Line Ladies FC, formed by a group of London Transport employees in the 1970s, which eventually merged with Wembley, taking on the latter's name and making the FA Cup Final in 1997; the other Barnet Ladies FC, established by men's club director Graham Slyper in the mid-1980s.

The two teams pooled their resources in 1998 under the Barnet umbrella, and London Bees were formed in 2014 to take a place in the newly-created WSL2. Officially the new club was separate to Barnet Ladies, but in practice much of the set-up simply moved over.

Gill Jones's involvement with the club stretches across four decades. As a teenager in 1975, she was thrilled to start playing for the District Line Ladies when she started work; although she would have loved to have played as a child, there simply wasn't an accessible club for her to join at the time. She became their club secretary and stayed in the role for much of the next 40 years – before the creation of London Bees.

In the summer of 2016, she wondered whether the organised way in which the club had been run had stood them in good stead for a Super League application and a shift to semi-professional football.

'We had a very good name in women's football,' she recalled. 'We were in the top flight of it, in the Women's Premier League for a number of years, so I think that all helped. It was a progression, really. All the personnel has changed now. Time goes on, we're not involved now on a day-to-day basis like we were before. We were all voluntary, and we'd all got other jobs, but now it's more full-time work and we're happy to step away from that.'

Barnet had helped out the Ladies throughout their time sharing their name, for which Jones was grateful.

'They supported us in everything: the kits, the playing facilities, everything we would have to pay out for they paid – but the players didn't get paid,' she said. 'The training venues, the playing venues, travel to away games, kits, equipment, league fees, county FA fees were all paid by Barnet. They were very good support, all those years.'

Jones also had some excellent memories of her lengthy playing career, including winning the WPL Cup and of one particular young team-mate at Wembley.

'Winning the WPL Cup as Wembley Ladies with Kelly Smith playing for us – she is the best ever player England have had,' declared Jones. 'I loved watching her, and to have her playing in my team, it was absolutely fantastic. That's something I'll always be pleased about – I had Kelly Smith in my team from when she was 14.'

Forty years on from her playing debut as an 18-year-old, Jones had seen women's football change significantly, and she was pleased that the London Bees players had such good facilities to access at The Hive. She did, however, sound a note of nostalgia about the impact of money on the game.

'It's getting to the stage where the more you can pay [the players], the better you're going to be,' she said. 'I think that's probably showing in WSL1 and gradually coming into WSL2 as well, I would think. The amount of money you're willing to pay – it's no different at the end of the day to men's football. It's going that way…it all becomes about money now, and that's a bit of a shame.'

※ ※ ※ ※ ※

With the size of the gaps between WSL fixtures, many clubs decided to arrange some friendly matches to keep themselves match-fit and ready.

Doncaster Belles had played only one WSL match since the start of the season in March, and in mid-April they thought that a behind-closed-doors friendly would be a good option to keep their newly-minted batch of full-time professionals poised for action.

Then news started to emerge that striker Courtney Sweetman-Kirk had picked up an injury during the game – and confirmation followed that she had broken her leg.

Ten days later, Sweetman-Kirk was in reasonably good spirits – and ready to talk about the incident, in her inimitably pragmatic style.

'We were just playing a behind-closed-doors friendly, and [it was] just a bit of a dodgy tackle really,' she said. 'It wasn't anything untoward or malicious, it was just a bit of a clumsy one, unfortunately, and I've come off the worst. I've been playing football for 20-odd years and I've always come off better, so it was my time, really, unluckily. It's just one of them things. Football: every time you step on the pitch it's a risk you take. I've been quite lucky for quite a few years, so unfortunately it's my time on the physio table.'

With her leg in plaster, she was just getting used to moving around on her crutches. She had already been updating her Twitter feed, announcing that she was being looked after by her parents – and her mother was washing her hair for her.

'I'm not too bad all things considered,' she said brightly – and then revealed that the break was a particularly serious one.

'I spent three days in hospital,' she said, adding that she had to undergo an operation to repair a comminuted fracture of the fibula which had also ruptured the ligaments around that bone. 'It wasn't a clean break. It was in four bits. So I've got a plate and a screw holding that together…I've got a pin going right across the ankle as well. It didn't go by halves. It definitely went the full whack.'

She was awaiting another hospital appointment to get her stitches removed. She had been expecting to be in plaster for six weeks, but was pleased that the hospital had agreed to put her in a lightweight protective boot after five and a half weeks – so she could board a plane and go on holiday at the end of May.

As an athlete, she was not used to sitting still, and was hoping that the chill British spring might warm up so that she could at least sun herself a little.

'Three times a day I've got simple exercises I'm doing at the minute, just to stop my quads and my hamstrings wasting away,' she said. She thought back to how she had spent her weekend – resting, immobile, in front of the television set. 'I've been quite lucky over the weekend, there's been loads of football on the telly. I love tennis as well, the Barcelona Masters was on and I love Rafa Nadal so I was watching him win that, so I was quite happy.'

One thing that was cheering her up was the mountain of 'get well' cards and messages she had received from fans and colleagues. Even though she lived a fair distance from Doncaster, one team-mate, Sophie Barker, based in Lincoln, had been able to drop in, but she was quick to thank everyone for taking the time to get in touch.

'Everyone has been in contact, calling me and messaging me, and I've been quite overwhelmed in terms of the amount of messages I've received, both privately and publicly and over social media. "Football family" is something that's used quite commonly, but I'd say that's how I feel – everyone has come together, it's nice to get those messages and it really does help with my recovery…I think I probably will struggle a bit, as every sportsperson does with big injuries, but that's the stuff I can look back on, keep my spirits up and it'll help me get through it.'

It was all an entirely new experience for Sweetman-Kirk, who had never suffered a serious injury before. In fact, she racked her brains and could not think of a single problem that had kept her out for more than one match at any point in her playing career, which stretched across two decades from junior to Women's Super League.

It was too early to make a prediction about when she might recover. With the metalwork holding her leg together, the healing process could be extensive, or it could be quick. Of course, for Sweetman-Kirk, the question mark was not just around when the bone would knit back together, but when she would be fully fit and strong enough to play again. She was intending to fully avail herself of the facilities of the National Health Service as well as the specialised rehabilitation care at the FA's St George's Park and, of course, the physiotherapy on offer at Doncaster Belles.

Ultimately, Sweetman-Kirk was sneakily pleased about the mid-season summer break that would normally disrupt her form – but would this year give her an extra few weeks to recuperate and the chance to play again before the end of the season.

'I'm normally cursing that summer break,' she confessed. 'It will give me the chance, second half of the season, [to] definitely aim to get back playing for that – probably towards the later half, but that's definitely an aim, I definitely want to get some games in. It's hard, the WSL fixtures, and the stop-start…but this season I'll be quite thankful for it – hoping that I can get back.'

We are Premier

A S the WSL settled as far as it could into its erratic routine, the rest of the domestic pyramid was drawing its scheduled fixtures to a close. The Women's Premier League was looking ahead to its promotion play-off, with the champions of their northern and southern divisions battling it out in a one-off game to step up to WSL2 in 2017, plus its imminent cup finals.

The WPL, although nominally part of the FA, is run by elected officials. Chairman Carol West, a police officer by profession, won her vote in 2014 when the women's game was restructured to create the second WSL2 division and allow for promotion from the WPL as well. It was a difficult election campaign, conducted amidst a climate of concern from the non-WSL clubs, worried they might be cast adrift as the governing body focused its efforts on a small number of elite teams. Fans were frightened too, launching social media campaigns to raise awareness of the changes to the system, and urging support for the WPL clubs as well as those further down the pyramid.

'There was a lot of unrest around the restructure, there was a campaign going, people really angry, they were quite frightened as well and unsure about the future,' admitted West. 'Because I'd been involved in the joint liaison committee with the other leagues, shaping what the new Premier League was going to look like, I was quite fortunate because I had a lot of information. I actually did an opening speech when I got voted in, it was quite embarrassing, stood in front of all these people, some of whom didn't really understand what was going on, and others were very angry. So I just stood there, really, and said, "This is who I am, this is what I can do, this is how I see it certainly for the first few years," and thankfully they gave me a go.'

In the two years since she took up her position, West had worked hard to create a new and distinct identity for the WPL.

'I'm quite resolute, I'm quite resilient, I'm quite determined, I don't take a job on if I'm not going to put everything into it, so it was a little bit of pressure to deliver,' she said. 'There's been some frustrations, it's fair to say, but overall we are trying to push the league on. That was part of what some people were frightened of, that it was just going to be forgotten about, it was just going to be thrown to the side. We have a mantra that says we control how big the gap between the Premier League and the Super League actually is.

'We've got to be realistic with that, of course, but regardless of what league I've been involved in, I've always looked forwards – see what they're doing, let's aspire to that standard, and, where we can, let's maintain that standard. That's what we've done. I think because they can see just how hard we work, how forward thinking we are, the kind of things we have brought in to develop the focus of the league, then by and large people have been quite supportive of it.'

In 2015, one of the initiatives brought in was an online TV channel featuring WPL match highlights – a pilot scheme, admittedly, but an exciting one – as well as a regular online magazine.

'What we didn't want was just the likes of a YouTube thing where people could just upload anything,' explained West.

'Last year we won the National Respect Award so we have to make sure the content's appropriate, and it's a standard as well – we're not just putting some poor footage on there, we're aspiring to a standard, so Karen [Falconer, the WPL development officer, a graphic designer in her day job] was all over the graphics to make it professional. It's just working with clubs: not everyone's got the facility to get it filmed or produce edited highlights. That's just a work in progress.

'Again, it's all about publicising, getting it out there, and showing our clubs that they've not been forgotten about, that we're actually keen to professionalise it. Certainly the clubs, in the north and south, they love it. That's where the buy-in comes from. We don't have the resources, unfortunately, that we'd like, but within the parameters that we can work in we do try to put things in place. We did start it as a pilot to invite a few clubs to get it off the ground, we will keep running with it – it just might change the format.'

West was clearly hugely engaged with her work in football, as was her colleague Falconer, both spending time travelling up and down from their homes to FA headquarters at Wembley Stadium for the required meetings. Indeed, West was managing this at the start of 2016 on crutches and with limited mobility after an operation on her leg – and all while maintaining her actual job. Serving as a league's elected official is a time-consuming responsibility.

'Obviously I work full-time but I've always got my iPad and my phone with me,' she pointed out, adding that although the FA provided link officials for the clubs, many felt happier talking to her simply because of their established relationship. 'We invite that open communication with clubs, so I can get e-mails from eight in the morning. I actually got a call at half past ten last night. From an availability point of view, it's pretty much 24 hours a day, and there's the work that goes in with that. It's like anything, if you want to do something well…'

She paused. 'I know some chairmen might want to sit back, delegate and let other people do stuff. I don't expect other people to do all the work while I'm just sat back.'

It certainly has been a lot of work since her tenure began. The WPL has had to create its own identity in the shadow of the WSL – but it has also had to ensure that its clubs are prepared should they approach the possibility of promotion, or if they are simply content to stay at their current level for the next few years. This kind of sustainability – and ensuring that everyone has the support they need – was challenging to guarantee.

West was sure some WPL clubs were already well organised enough to make the jump up – with players who could genuinely compete.

'Obviously the Super League is set up with an application process, and some teams quite rightly went there – they were in a position where they're very strong around playing strength. And why not? Fantastic – but as with any application process, sometimes they might fit the criteria in terms of the infrastructure of the club, but on the playing strength of it, I think that's sometimes where the two disconnect.

'Looking at the teams that we've got, you look at Charlton, they used to be Croydon, you've got big names like Brighton, and Sheffield are up there [in WSL2], holding their own, although it's early days yet, so I don't think it's really the players, because the Premier League's always had good players. Certainly in WSL2, player for player I think they can probably match them. Club for club, if you take the best of our players from the north and south and 99 per cent of WSL2, I think they can hold their own, to be fair.'

She pointed to the recent FA Cup quarter-finals, where WPL side Sporting Club Albion had taken on WSL1 giants Manchester City. She did also wonder, however, whether the day would come when a club eligible for promotion to WSL2 would not fulfil the licensing criteria – or even decide not to take it up because they could not afford the investment in off-the-pitch infrastructure, even with whatever FA support was offered.

'Just because you want to do it, doesn't mean that you can,' she said. 'Obviously there are quite stringent criteria that you've got to meet.

'Drilling down, it's not the fact that you might have got the best team that goes out week in week out and beats the other teams, it's what you've got behind that, and some clubs just don't have it.

'In the Premier League we've got a real spectrum. We've got the likes of Brighton, who are backed by the men's club, they've got all of that, they've got people who are being paid, people being employed by the club to actually make that, whereas within the same division you've got clubs that are perhaps running with three people, and it's the volunteers coming in, self-financing, doing all of that stuff, so just because you do well on the pitch, it doesn't automatically mean they're going to get promoted.'

There was a sense of sadness from West around the entire play-off concept. With the WPL organised into two regional leagues, one of the season's champions would end up ultimately disappointed while seeing the other leap up into the big time. Brighton had just secured their place in the play-off as southern champions, and were waiting to find out who they would be playing against.

'It is exciting but it's obviously quite cruel as well,' she said. 'The Premier League, albeit it's been restructured, it's been there for many many years, and the teams that are actually now in the northern and southern division have actually come through the pyramid, and it's obviously taken them year on year to do that.

'We know from today that Brighton will be in that, they'll be joined by our northern champions – and it's fantastic, it's winner takes all, but the other side of it – your entire hopes and aspirations are dashed by the fact you've lost that particular football match. But…that's football.'

※ ※ ※ ※ ※

The WPL's cup finals spread themselves across almost a month, with the Plate Final held at Hednesford Town FC at the end of April.

It was the first national cup final for Enfield Town, and the first Plate Final for Coventry United, ensuring a double piece of history for whoever won.

It turned out to be Coventry of the Premier League Southern Division, taking their lower-league opponents apart in the second half after a rather even opening 45 minutes to secure a 5-1 win.

Crissy Torkildsen picked up the player of the match award for her impressive display, holding the ball up brilliantly and having a hand in all five goals. In fact, the scoresheet recorded her name as the scorer of one – but she admitted she had not got the final touch to any.

'They've given me a goal, but no,' she said. 'I was involved in all of them, but didn't actually score myself. I definitely didn't get a touch.'

Torkildsen was proud of the way her team had competed, regrouping at half-time to assert themselves, and dealing with Enfield, who were something of an unknown quantity.

'It was a bit nerve-wracking for some of the girls that had never been involved in a final – not really knowing what to expect from Enfield because of where they're at, them being a league below, where they're at in the table, not knowing too much about them,' she said. 'I just think they're always going to battle, that's what you get from London teams. And they did, they put us on our back foot a little bit. We were quite nervous, definitely for the first half-hour at least, but then second half, once we got into our stride and just sorted out a few things at half-time, we were finally starting to dominate the ball, get in behind them, create opportunities, and as soon as we scored the third goal, to be honest, we just looked like we were going to keep scoring. It was quite comfortable, then.'

She was pleased with her own display, although she had some of the bruises to prove it, having been the recipient of a few crunching tackles as Enfield tried to rob her of possession, and describing her performance, 'I held the ball up when I needed to, I played it simple when I needed to, and I drew fouls when I was getting chopped.'

It was very different to the way she had played a few weeks before against Tottenham Hotspur, just below them in the table, and the team to take away their unbeaten home record in the league – with the caveat that the game was not at Coventry's usual home ground at Stratford, instead held at Rugby Town.

'We lost to Spurs, 2-1 a couple of weeks ago, which was disappointing,' she recalled. 'We had a lot of chances – I personally should have scored at least three, just one of those days in front of goal. We couldn't finish, we lost focus, got a bit tired. It's that time of the year. They scored two quick goals in 15 minutes, and they're a good side, I know a lot of the girls who play there, and they've got a very good team spirit, which helped them in that game, because they kept going and then they managed to get a couple of goals. It was disappointing from our point of view because we should have done much better, but that's football for you.'

Torkildsen, at the age of 30, had moved down to play in the WPL after some years at Birmingham Ladies of the WSL. During her spell there, she had played at the very highest club level, the UEFA Women's Champions League, but ultimately WSL football did not suit her. She was feeling physically fatigued after moving straight from the WSL summer season to the WPL winter season without a break – and she was not the only one in the Coventry squad suffering. With their excellent cup run plus their league fixtures, their calendar had got rather congested, and players were feeling the strain.

'We've got quite a small squad at the minute, which we are looking to improve for next year: a lot of people are playing a lot of minutes,' she said. 'I came [to Coventry] in October, so I'd been playing non-stop for 18 months. I physically feel very tired – from that point of view I haven't had a break from football.'

Torkildsen had found herself on the fringes of the Birmingham squad, meaning she was not getting regular games while she was there, despite the amount of training sessions in which the entire squad participated.

'I wasn't playing much at Blues – it felt like you were, because we were training three, four times, in-house games against boys' teams, which for me personally was amazing, but actually in a league sense and the cup sense I was only getting a handful of games,' she explained. 'I got to the point where I just got frustrated, and you could see that. Things had changed for me. I'd been at Blues for a long time, but I'd had a spell at Cov for a year when we got promoted, years and years ago, so I knew it was a good club. They look after people.

'The core of the team that I left four years ago was still there, and they're very young – they were VERY young when I was there the first time, now they're still only 24, 34, so I know they've got a good base to build from, and that's what I want. I want to go to a club that's ambitious and wants to succeed and wants to push on to Super League. That's why I went there. There's a lot of things we need to do as a club, but my involvement as a player and maybe my experience was the reasons I went to Cov.'

She was not impressed by the WSL fixture scheduling, which she felt had a negative effect on the players' form and quality of matches – but also on attendances.

'There's no continuity. I support a men's team and I look forward to it, I check if they're home or away, I watch them on Sky: [following a WSL team] you don't get any of that because you're thinking, "They're not playing for another four weeks," so that continuity has disappeared.

'I think there's too many breaks, and [as a player] you feel like you're in a pre-season constantly. If you have a game and then have four weeks off, you have to keep your fitness up and you're not playing games. You feel like you're in pre-season at least three times across a Super League season, which for me isn't good for morale – the schedule for me doesn't work. I don't think that influenced my minutes [on the pitch at Birmingham], but at the same time none of us could get a consistent run of games and get form, and that might have impacted on being picked or not – but I wasn't playing anyway, I was just a squad player.'

Torkildsen was reflective on the impact that the introduction of the Women's Super League had had on the Women's Premier League – but also on young players' development.

'WSL2 are pulling a lot of the better players from the Premier League up there, even the young ones, even the young players in the development squads [the youth/reserve set-up],' she said. 'They should be playing Premier League football or being involved in those clubs, but they stay in development because that's a Super League team – which is fine if that's what they want to do, but…there needs to be more and better players that want to progress through the pathway at Premier League standard. Then you hopefully would be able to give a 17-, 18-, 19-year-old an opportunity to play some minutes – in women's football.'

Torkildsen spoke from another level of experience as well – she was coaching girls and young women, who she felt would do better and progress more by playing against other women rather than sticking with the youth set-up.

'That's what some of them girls need: playing women's football is different from playing youth football,' she said.

During the day she worked for Birmingham County FA as a football development officer, part of the children and young people team working to increase participation, mostly in an education setting. Her employers had been very understanding when her Super League contract required her to train on weekdays, but she had never intended to become a professional footballer, simply because the WSL launch had come a little too late in her playing career for her to take that risk.

'I had to work because of my age and where I'm at in my career – I can't just go into it full time,' she said.

In the meantime, she was pursuing her real love, coaching, working in a centre of excellence and completing her UEFA A Licence qualification so she could ultimately move into that as a full-time job. She talked with infectious enthusiasm about her enjoyment of coaching, concluding, 'That's my passion.'

※ ※ ※ ※ ※

The pleasantly Proustian aroma of a coal-fired train filled the air at Kidderminster. As morning turned to afternoon, a small group of people disembarked the nearby branch line, which connected the town to Birmingham.

A young man in a blazer asked an older man in a football club-crested tie for directions to Aggborough. It transpired he was the fourth official for the afternoon's FA Women's Premier League Cup Final – and the stadium official was happy to guide him through the new housing estate next to the station, a shortcut to the ground.

Aggborough is positioned between a residential street and a railway line, with a capacity of around 6,500. It has previously hosted men's junior internationals, as the stadium official boasted, and they were looking forward to welcoming the women's game for one of the showpiece end-of-season events.

It was a perfect day for football as well. Inside the stadium, as the sun beat down with a pleasant breeze swirling across the stands, the groundsman was putting the final touches to the pitch, mixing the smell of freshly cut grass with the nearby steam train. Meanwhile, the staff in charge of the stadium sound system were testing out the speakers, ensuring the national anthems were ready – 'Hen Wlad Fy Nhadau' for Cardiff City, and 'God Save The Queen' for Tottenham Hotspur.

The representatives of the governing body greeted each other, with officials from the FA meeting with the WPL's West and Falconer. It was Falconer, who was given credit for the excellent displays of WPL branding around the ground – a PVC banner behind each goal, all the better for the footage of the match highlights, and flags around the tunnel, two with the FA crest, and four with the WPL badge.

Both of them were thrilled about their weekend so far, which had started the day before with a presentation at Crystal Palace's Selhurst Park. At half-time in the men's game between Palace and Stoke City, they had given the WPL Division One (south-east) trophy to the women's team, and met with a rousing reception. All four sides of the ground – including the visiting fans – had applauded the women's achievement, and welcomed their lap of honour. There were no heckles, nor a lack of interest; there was a delight in the achievements of a group of dedicated footballers, regardless of their club allegiance.

At Aggborough, the Cardiff squad were the first to head out to get a feel for the conditions, walking around the pitch and assessing the ground – beautifully green across most of the playing area, with some sand on the touchline and in the goalmouths.

The referee and his assistants did the same shortly afterwards, and were followed by the Tottenham players. There was a tangible feeling of excitement, even before the gates opened to admit the spectators; the players were noisy, laughing, and both squads took the opportunity to cluster together for ambitious selfies.

The players' families were gathering already, proudly snapping pictures of their daughters as the team coaches went through the pre-match pleasantries, shaking hands with the dignitaries. Loud chart music accompanied the warm-ups as fans filtered in, quickly ushered away from the directors' box area and into the neighbouring blocks of seats. It soon became obvious why – both squads had brought plenty of volunteers and staff with them, and they had reserved those particular places.

The refreshment kiosk near the turnstiles was doing brisk business. A local girls' team, 22 players from Wyre Forest Phoenix in full kit, began a walk round the perimeter of the pitch, all the better to take up their position as ball girls after kick-off. They just missed being caught by the pitch sprinklers, which sprang into action to dampen the somewhat dry sidelines. Bottled water was the order of the day for the squads, readying themselves for the warm conditions.

Cardiff also welcomed to the pitch their mascot for the afternoon – the four-year-old nephew of captain Abbie Britton. He and his family had travelled up from Bristol that morning, and the little boy was in his element running around and joining in part of the goalkeepers' warm-up. As his dad accompanied him back to the stands, the girls' team filed out of the tunnel to form a guard of honour for the squads as they headed back to the changing rooms for their last pep talk before kick-off. The girls waved their purple WPL flags, fluttering pleasingly in the breeze.

The stadium announcer read out the teams, and, as often happens at these kinds of games, it became very clear where each player's friends and family were sitting as cheers rang out in different places across the stand after each name. There was a scattering of replica shirts around the ground too, indicating club allegiances as well as support for loved ones.

West herself took the trophy to the pitch, placing it on a plinth just by the tunnel, so all the players walked past it as they lined up to shake her hand, and then for the anthems – played for real this time, and both observed largely impeccably by all. After a quick huddle and the customary exchange of pennants by the captains, then a minute's silence to commemorate Victory in Europe day – during which the only sound was bird song plus intermittent imitations indicating the arrival of a text message somewhere in the ground – it was time for the afternoon's serious business to begin.

It was a hugely entertaining game, worthy of a cup final. Both sides were committed to good attacking play, with Tottenham more threatening from open play and Cardiff putting on the pressure down the flanks to force set pieces. With such industry on show, it was no surprise that water breaks were necessary throughout as players and officials alike took every opportunity to rehydrate themselves. Tottenham's Bianca Baptiste was a physical threat, luring the Cardiff defence into fouls, but her best chance of the first half came as a one-on-one, saved well by keeper Alesha McGlynn – that was, until the half-hour, when she followed Leah Rawle's attempted lob up excellently to slam the ball into the roof of the net from close range. Hope Souminen grabbed a spectacular equaliser on the very stroke of half-time, though, beautifully chipping Toni-Ann Wayne to level things up.

As legs tired, the play got slightly scrappier, with long, lofted balls forward. With no more goals in the second half, it was into 30 minutes of extra time. Nerves were evident around the ground as the teams gathered to receive their instructions from their coaches – who shook hands once more as the referee Darren McMillain blew his whistle for the resumption of the game. Wendy Martin thought she had put Tottenham back in front, but assistant referee Kat Davey had long had her flag raised for offside.

For a large portion of the second half, the skies had clouded over; as the final reached its denouement, the sun broke through once more. Yet for Cardiff it looked set to be a dark day as goalkeeper McGlynn took a nasty blow to the face, falling to the ground and eventually having to be helped off towards the end of the first period of extra time with her face covered in blood. They had already used all three of their substitutes, meaning Hannah Mills bravely stepped up, swapping her blue shirt for the yellow one and taking McGlynn's gloves as the stricken keeper walked slowly and gingerly back down the tunnel, supported on either side by backroom staff.

Tottenham piled the pressure on while Cardiff packed their back line, protecting their stand-in custodian, hoping they could cling on for the drama of a penalty shoot-out. The ten women could not last, though; in the very last minute of extra time, Maya Vio got the final touch from a corner to score past Mills. The celebrations from the dugout spilled out briefly on to the pitch, before the coaching staff gathered themselves and took their seats again for the remaining seconds.

When the whistle blew, the Cardiff players sank to the turf. They could not have given any more. The Tottenham team, meanwhile, were delirious, lifting Vio to their collected shoulders. The presentation podium was quickly put together, with medals given to the match officials first. Touchingly, as the runners-up wiped their disappointed tears away and prepared to line up to collect their medals, the ones which nobody had wanted, the champions calmed down and formed a respectful guard of honour, applauding each of their opponents.

Cardiff returned the compliment as Tottenham collected their medals and captain Jenna Schillaci lifted the trophy.

Champagne – in bottles marked with the competition logo – was sprayed everywhere, and the Welsh side made as swift an exit as they could manage.

Captain Britton immediately put her medal around the neck of her small nephew. 'It's nice to see so many people supporting the women's game as well,' she added. 'It's growing. He loves it. I'm glad he was here.'

Clearly exhausted after 120 minutes of strenuous draining cup final football, she was disappointed but quick to pay tribute to her players. She revealed that one had picked up a hamstring pull, forcing her to be substituted in normal time, and another had felt a twang during extra time, meaning that for the last 15 minutes they were effectively playing with nine.

'I'm so proud of them, so, so proud of them,' she said. She had not thought that the corner which led to the goal should have been awarded, but accepted the decision anyway.

'I think when we went into the second phase of extra time, we would have taken penalties,' Britton said, and added that she thought in the last 15 minutes Tottenham had been the better team. 'Credit to Tottenham – they did well and kept going, just like we would have.'

Britton was based in Exeter, and worked full-time in office administration, travelling to Cardiff once a week for training.

'It's all worth it – unfortunately not on days like today,' she said. 'But it is worth it when you do win and you play well and you've got all the girls around you.'

Her opposite number, Tottenham's Schillaci, was so delighted that she could barely express it.

'It's absolutely amazing, I can't really believe it!' she said. 'We worked so hard. We deserve it. I'm so proud of every single player. We played two finals already, and last week we lost. We could have easily dropped our heads but we've come back stronger and finally we've got the trophy we wanted.'

First-team manager Karen Hills was more measured but equally happy with her players.

'Credit to the girls, I thought they were fantastic today,' she said. 'Their work rate was excellent, the belief was there, they kept going right to the end.'

She was swift to ask about the wellbeing of McGlynn and send Tottenham's best wishes to her, even in the midst of the celebration, and paid tribute to Cardiff and everyone who was part of the occasion.

'I thought it was a great spectacle of women's football – the atmosphere was good,' she said. 'We'll regroup, review the season – everyone's just going to have a bit of a break over the next couple of weeks. Then we start again, obviously building on what we've already done this season, continuing the momentum, and hope we're in the same position next season.'

She was cautious about the rumour that the women would get to play at the men's famous ground at some point in 2016/17.

'There have been people speaking about it, but nothing's been cemented, nothing's been confirmed,' she said, before adding with a smile, 'If we do, it'll be fantastic for the ladies and obviously being the last season at White Hart Lane it'll be part of history.'

In the bar afterwards, the Cardiff players remained subdued. Stand-in goalkeeper Mills had two fingers taped up; she had broken them when she made her first save, batting the ball away and catching her hand awkwardly. The news on McGlynn was limited; a broken nose was suspected plus a cut on her face that would require stitches or gluing.

There was not too much time to wallow or celebrate, really; extra time had drained both squads and they had to get on the coaches back home. After all, they had to go to work in the morning.

※ ※ ※ ※ ※

The following weekend, Abbie Britton was walking down the high street for a spot of Saturday morning shopping. She had come to terms with the cup final defeat, even if some of her team-mates hadn't.

'There's a couple that are still really hurting,' she said. 'They're disappointed. A lot of them – they won't mind me saying it – it probably will have been their last cup final, there's a few old heads in this squad.'

That included Michelle Green, the most capped Wales international ever, who had made an early exit from the game at Kidderminster due to a hamstring pull. Painful as it was, hers was not the most serious injury incurred by the Cardiff players; Alesha McGlynn was still suffering from the boot she had taken to the face, with her vision impaired.

Britton's job as captain was to raise the squad's spirits one more time that season, for their final WPL Southern Division game against Coventry, bringing together the mix of youth and vast experience in the side.

'I look at it as a bit of an honour, to be honest with you,' she reflected. 'Gemma Evans, who's a very good central defender, who's just broken into the senior team now – she's phenomenal. When they mould her, when she gets more experience, she's going to be one for the future. Then there's Michelle Green, the most capped Welsh player ever, she's been in the game since most of us were in nappies. That experience helps. She's not very vocal, she's not one to scream her head off but when Mush speaks, people listen. It's a good blend to have.

'When I'm stuck and I don't know what to say or I don't quite know what the best solution is to things, I look to her and I look to the youngsters as well to know what they want. I'm not very vocal on the pitch, I do my talking through playing, I don't like to shout, or point fingers, I try and encourage them all the time, and I think that's the best way, really.'

Nobody at Britton's office had taken much interest in what she'd done the previous weekend, but she was used to that. In her previous job, she had worked for the city council, who had been much more supportive.

'My previous job, when I was living in Cardiff, the council were very interested in it, and freed me up to allow me to go to training and things like that,' she recalled. 'Now I have to use more of my own time, and you can understand why they do that as their business, but it is hard, you've got to find the right balance between work and social life, because they're just as important as each other. It's not the easiest. I'd be lying if I said it was.'

Would her employers have a different view were she a man playing at an equivalent level? She sighed at a question that female footballers often find themselves answering, even in 2016.

'Definitely,' she replied, pointing to the reasonable money on offer to players at the top end of non-league men's football. 'They're slowly introducing money into women's football, but it won't be introduced to the men's level ever, I don't think, which is obviously a great shame.'

Britton talked about the continuing debate about how much female athletes should get paid – decades after equal pay in other industries had been agreed. In early 2016, tennis star Novak Djokovic had found himself embroiled in a discussion about whether or not his female equivalents should also get the same prize money as him should they win a tournament; Indian Wells tournament chief Raymond Moore suggested not, because of the broader commercial pull of the top male stars.

'Why shouldn't they earn just as much?' asked Britton rhetorically. 'I understand that they maybe get bigger crowds, but [the female tennis players] apply themselves and do just the same amount as training as men. Their commitment is just as big – same as ours. I sometimes question whether or not the professionals have the same commitment as the non-professionals and the lower-league players. They get it all given on a plate. We still have to pay to play, you know? Our commitment is through the roof because we pay to do it.'

Britton was critical about the ways in which elite women's football was marketed, suggesting that it was still a minority sport because of the lack of media coverage – but with better reporting and better advertising, more money would enable better pay for players at the top end of the game. In return, those players would be able to concentrate on their football, not worry about making ends meet. Of course, potential sponsors would only be attracted if there was already media promotion and a captive audience on offer. It was the eternal paradox of women's football; a vicious circle in a capitalist system.

She had mixed feelings even about the 500 people watching the WPL Cup Final at Aggborough, describing it as 'obviously fantastic', adding, 'A lot of the girls haven't played in front of bigger crowds than that. Then you've got one or two who've played in front of 50 or 60 thousand. The comparison is huge. Will you ever get [crowds of several hundred] in that league? I don't think so. *Should* you get it in that league? I think so.'

In the meantime, Britton was just focused on her own team. She wondered whether a team based in Wales would be allowed promotion to the WSL should they ever win the national WPL championship, but acknowledged it was moot until they topped the table. Cardiff found themselves battling with WSL clubs for players, with Yeovil, Bristol City and Reading all in the same broad catchment area.

'Obviously the attraction of WSL football is a big thing for players, and you can't fault them – they want to better themselves and they want to go and taste it and experience it,' she said. 'I have no question in my mind that if we were a WSL team we'd have a lot of Bristol, Yeovil, maybe even Reading players in and among the squad, because it's such a big club, it's massive.'

She speculated that having a Welsh team in the WSL would also give the Wales national team a boost, but quickly added, 'All this is irrelevant until we win the league, and that is the be-all and end-all, really.

'It's out of our hands until we win it. Unfortunately for the last two years we've fallen quite short – not just short, *quite* short. We just need to do our job on the pitch and not worry about what's going on in the back room. Then when we do win it, which hopefully is next season, then we can ask those questions.'

Dreams

THE road to Wembley was in sight for four WSL1 teams in mid-April. After Manchester City had dispatched Sporting Club Albion – the WPL's final representative – in the quarter-finals, it was a top-flight affair for the FA Women's Cup semi-finals.

Sunderland took on Arsenal at Meadow Park, a long distance to travel on a Sunday afternoon – and it was a day when the Gunners' men's side were also playing at home, reducing the crowd even further to a touch over 900. As always, the club made some effort to entertain the younger fans, with their regular tent set up with art supplies plus word puzzles. Today there was a face-painter on hand, a semi-regular occurrence, although she had not been there for the previous home game.

On that day, the Arsenal club mascot Gunnersaurus – a large green dinosaur in full kit – had been meeting and greeting the youngsters; today he was nowhere to be seen, presumably a few miles closer to London at the Emirates Stadium instead.

There were also two trophies on display in the ground – the Continental Cup, which the team had won in 2015, and the FA Under-17s Cup, which the juniors had won the day before. The FA Women's Cup itself was on show outside the ground at the main entrance – those going through those turnstiles had the chance to take pictures with it, while those at the other end of the ground remained blissfully unaware that it was there at all.

There was a noisy travelling contingent, though, setting up camp on the terraces on both sides of the pitch, and in the opening stages they had plenty to cheer. Emma Mitchell's dismissal just after the half-hour mark for a second bookable offence pleased them, giving them the numerical advantage with the score still goalless.

As so often happens, though, the ten-player team were revitalised. Danielle van de Donk scored the first goal six minutes later after a scramble on the line, and Dan Carter got the second on 55 minutes, turning in Natalia's cross.

The numbers were evened up 15 minutes from time when Abby Holmes was sent off for fouling van de Donk – the Sunderland player's second red card in as many games at Meadow Park. Once it was ten against ten, the home side were rampant. Fara Williams converted the penalty, Carter added another to her tally, Jordan Nobbs got one, and van de Donk scored twice more to complete her hat-trick and an absolute rout.

The other semi-final was a slightly closer affair with Manchester City leading Chelsea by a solitary Jane Ross goal until the closing moments when the reigning PFA Player of the Year Ji So Yun equalised with a free kick. Extra time followed and Fran Kirby left it late to snatch the winner.

There were plenty more people at Wheatsheaf Park to see the match, though – 2,278 in attendance with a sizeable away support. That was thanks in part to Manchester City's efforts, laying on complimentary travel for travelling fans on the Sunday morning; and in part to the scheduling of the men's Premier League, which had thrown up the same fixture on the previous evening, meaning that City fans could stay in the capital overnight and see the women the next day.

So both home sides secured their places in the final – and triggered a debate about whether any side should have home advantage in such an important knockout game. City's captain Steph Houghton was understandably disappointed and suggested that cup semi-finals of this nature should be played at a neutral venue, just as happens in the men's game – and indeed, had happened in the Women's FA Cup previously. In 2015, Everton had played Notts County at Goodison Park – the home of the men's team – and Chelsea had taken on Manchester City at Adams Park, a venue much used by the FA for high-profile women's matches, and the home ground of Wycombe Wanderers.

'You've got quite a short period between the quarter-finals and the semi-finals to find a venue, which is difficult to find at this time of year because a lot of [men's] clubs have got a backlog of fixtures, or they're protecting their ground for key fixtures coming up,' explained the FA's Kelly Simmons. 'You've then got to promote it to the locality and try and get fans there – when fans in that drive-time area aren't necessarily the ones who'd go to watch women's football. So it becomes quite a hard thing to promote.

'Ultimately we want to move the semi-finals on to television. Talking to the clubs, it'll be better to put it on a home venue so you've got the venue sorted straight away; the club can use it to really generate a really good crowd; revenues go back into women's football rather than a standalone club somewhere that you've booked in terms of tickets but also the secondary spend.

'It's a risk, I think; [if] you're desperately trying to market that game in the [neutral] area and trying to get a reasonable level of fans, I think it's just too risky to try and get that game televised and try and take it to a wider audience. We're open-minded – I've seen that some players don't like it and some do. We'll see how it goes – talk to them at the end of the season and see what they think.'

※ ※ ※ ※ ※

While Arsenal and Chelsea prepared for a London derby at Wembley in the FA Cup Final, there was a very different local clash taking place at a school in Islington.

A gym on the second floor of a secondary school is the home for a women's indoor league on a Tuesday evening, and in April the two teams from Goaldiggers clashed, offering those who were apprehensive about actually playing in a match rather than simply going through their training drills, the new and the nervous, the chance to make their debuts in a friendly, non-threatening environment. One of the players there for the first time was almost overflowing with excitement – partially for the game, partially for her brand-new, bright orange boots and shin pads, of which she was very proud.

As with so many small-sided leagues, the position of goalkeeper was a rotating one, with the communal gloves shared around. What was less usual, however, was the utter lack of complaining when switched into the keeper's role, or when substituted to give someone else some playing time. It was a uniquely supportive atmosphere, with applause around the hall both for good play and good intentions.

After the game, as per normal, the players gathered in the school reception area to listen to coach Ruby Marlow's feedback on the performance, with a medal awarded to her players of the match.

One was Fleur Cousens, the club's founder and driving force.

A few days later, she was still delighted about the success of that particular evening – not her own performance, but the way the squads had come together, and the bravery of those playing in a match for the first time.

'I think quite a lot [of the players] are just – not too scared, but they want to join the league when they think they can,' she explained. 'We don't want to pressurise anyone to be in a match until they want to be.'

The teams for each match were organised a few days beforehand based on players' availability; a post on the club's Facebook page asked members to click the 'like' button if they wanted to play in the game, on a first-come first-served basis.

'I think some of them have this idea in their head of letting down the team if they don't think they're good enough,' she added. 'It's not really about the winning, it's more about getting everyone to take part because that's the best practice in many ways.

'It's nice because at training there's always a good core of people, which is good,' she was quick to point out, 'and then some people are really into the matches and they prefer to do that.'

In such a supportive environment there was also an additional problem – those who were confident with playing in matches were worried that they might be being greedy if they volunteered themselves too much, taking away the chance for someone else to have a go.

It had its advantages, though. The closeness of the group and its camaraderie led to situations such as the applause for good play, good technique or simply a good idea from both sets of players when the two Goaldiggers teams faced off against each other.

'So many people haven't played before, and we all know what we've been working on, so if something happens as a direct result of something we've been going through, you're like, "Yay, well done!"' she said. 'It's quite exciting to see it in game play.'

With the increasing numbers, they were considering how they might accommodate more players in the future and enable them to get game time – although entering an 11-a-side league was a pipe dream.

'Possibly we'll have to find a seven-a-side league,' Cousens speculated. 'Eleven-a-side, I 100 per cent want to enter, but maybe in two years when everyone's confident enough. That's a whole new ball game. We'll definitely keep going. Maybe we'll have our own league one day!'

The financial problems the club were facing, however, had not improved in the intervening months. A funding sub-committee had been set up with the task of raising money, and the ultimate aim was to come up with a way to keep the club running while maintaining affordable membership fees. Cousens was keen to get hold of kits for the new members; when the local pub had agreed to sponsor them, Goaldiggers had only 40 players, so they bought 50 kits to be on the safe side.

'It's a bit annoying now because we have more people who want to be members – we didn't envisage that,' she said. 'It'll be a bit of a shame to be a member and not have the beautiful kit. Members find an excuse to wear it! Showing it round at work – it makes you feel extra proud of your team.'

Players were even planning to bring their friends and family along to matches, just to show off what they could do; and wanting to impress their onlookers, they were carefully choosing games in which they were confident the Goaldiggers would put up a decent display and have a good chance of winning – or at least scoring goals.

'The girls are just amazing,' said Cousens, reflecting on the utter commitment and enthusiasm of the club's players. 'It's hard to find a new sport and they're having to play in an expensive league. I'm so impressed how they all take it in their stride – one kick at a time.'

※ ※ ※ ※ ※

Every Goaldiggers player found it difficult to speak highly enough of their coaches, Josh Pugh and Ruby Marlow. With so many players they had plenty to do, splitting the workload between training and working with a team during their formal matches in the league.

'They're like the glue of the club,' said Cousens. 'They're amazing. They always go that extra mile.'

The players were especially complimentary about Marlow. They saw her as a role model and as a footballing inspiration.

'Have you seen our coach Ruby play?' asked one player. 'She's REALLY good.'

Marlow had spent her teenage years playing for Tottenham Hotspur Ladies, now an established WPL club.

'I've always been interested in football,' she explained. At primary school, she asked why there was no team for her to play in, and that forced them to create one.

'I was doing so well there that the teacher said, "You should be going somewhere else," and that's when she put me through to start playing for Tottenham Ladies. That's what I did all through my secondary school life.'

When it came to considering her higher education options, she was faced with a tough decision. She could potentially study in America, aiming for a sports scholarship and focusing on her football; or she could stay in the UK and take a more academic path in life. In the end, she opted to study for a degree in sports development at Teesside University, where she played for the university team.

After graduation, she returned to London and began to work towards her coaching badges, which she found were increasingly important to work in the sport sector. Working with the Goaldiggers women was a step towards that, and coaching them was something Marlow evidently enjoyed. She was full of praise in return for Cousens's sheer industry.

'When I arrived, it was such a pleasant atmosphere to be part of, and I think that Fleur really radiates all of that herself. She's such a great person, and it's so inspiring to look at all the work she's been doing. I think it's the mix, all the girls coming together and we're all wanting to try. They're all trying this new thing – some of the girls have never even kicked a ball before, and I just think everyone is so supportive, and it's such a nice place to be that we're all just wanting everyone to do as well as they can.'

Having said that, she had found herself trying new methods of coaching, because dealing with beginner players at adult level is self-evidently very different from working with children.

'The first training session [at Goaldiggers] was quite weird for me, because up until that point I'd never really coached girls or women, all I've been coaching was small boys, so it was weird to be then coaching people my age but also women as well. It was a new challenge for me as well, starting coaching this team, but it was a good one as well, a different experience, one I really enjoy.'

One of the major differences Marlow highlighted was the lack of history with the game that many women had when compared to small boys, who were brought up watching and playing football almost by right.

'It's a completely different thing. You're going straight back to the basics. Even though I'm coaching boys, they've been kicking a football for a lot longer than these women have been kicking a football, so you're having to coach the basics. You're having to talk to them differently but they're also taking it on a lot quicker. It's really interesting to watch.'

While coaching was her focus, and a career she wanted to develop even further, she had spent the previous months working as a barista to pay the bills, with the added bonus that the hours were flexible, leaving her evenings free to work with her teams. She had just taken a job at a local school, which she was hoping would give her the opportunity to work with teams there.

'It also allows me to get my weekends free so I can possibly start playing myself, which I've not been able to do since I got back from uni,' she said, clearly very happy with the prospect. 'There's a really nice mixed gender staff football match every Friday as well, which I've just started doing – so even though it's not club level, it's really nice to start kicking a ball myself as well.'

She was also hoping that in the future she would be able to use her sports development degree in a more direct way as part of her career. She knew from her own experience that female football coaches working with other women and girls had the potential to really make a difference.

'I would really like to use that with my coaching qualifications to focus more on girls' football, grassroots level, because I know how important it is,' she said. 'I never had someone like me to look up to when I was younger. Right now I coach a lot of football but the majority of it is boys' football, and I look at what I'm doing and I think that I'm... not wasted on the boys, but I feel that they could easily have another coach, someone that's not me.

'I know how important it is for girls and women to be doing this sport, and I know that I can be such a help with that, and that's why I think I should be focusing more on girls' football, which is what I'm trying to do.'

Summer 2016

London calling

NEITHER Arsenal nor Chelsea had far to travel for the 2016 Women's FA Cup Final, hosted at Wembley for the second year running. Emma Hayes, the Chelsea manager, had said she was hoping for 50,000 fans there, which would have almost doubled the attendance from a year previously.

The merchandise stands were out early, set out in the car parks of the pubs nearby. One offered a baby's romper suit, emblazoned with the words 'Me and my dad love Arsenal'; questionable grammar aside, it was fascinating to see the assumption that it would be fathers bringing their children to any football match, let alone one competed between women.

Actually, this game saw many parents bringing their youngsters. With the sponsorship of SSE, the energy company, the FA were able to offer free tickets to children. There were plenty of coach trips, children's teams making the journey to the national stadium, but also a lot of families. From noon the stands began to fill; fans packed the Wembley lower tier, with flags distributed to make the scene a riot of colour. Although segregation was not rigorously enforced, the general idea was to separate the fans out with Arsenal supporters behind one goal and Chelsea behind the other, creating an exciting and partisan atmosphere.

To that end, each side had an on-pitch interviewer of their own, taking over the tannoy for part of the pre-match warm-up to get the fans at each end going, much like the warm-up act or a support band at a gig. Indeed, the stadium was much like a gig at times, with DJ Lilah Parsons running the music from pitchside for a spell. It developed into a party at points, with everyone joining in the waves, rising to their feet and lifting their arms as it circled the stands.

Before they led their teams out, Hayes and her counterpart Pedro Martinez Losa shook hands in the tunnel, both smart in their suits and with the traditional cup final buttonhole. Accompanied by a squad of mascots, the players walked out into the north London sunshine, and lined up respectfully for the national anthem – performed by musical theatre star Samantha Barks, Eponine in the West End and Oscar-winning film productions of *Les Misérables*, and more recently seen on television alongside Arsenal captain Alex Scott as they took on the survival challenge posed by Bear Grylls's latest reality show.

Arsenal – 13-time holders of the trophy – went in as underdogs against the double winners, but their performance did not reflect that. From the off they were dominant, and when Dan Carter chipped Hedwig Lindahl magnificently from the edge of the box after 17 minutes it was no less than they deserved. The entire display was masterminded brilliantly by the legendary Kelly Smith, finally fully match fit after so many injuries keeping her out for so long; her vision was exemplary.

Katie Chapman and Gemma Davison – former Arsenal players both – worked their hardest but could not get Chelsea back into it. Even Ji So Yun and Fran Kirby, two stars who had so often been compared to the likes of Lionel Messi for their style of play, were kept relatively quiet by a solid centre-back pairing comprising Casey Stoney and Germany international Josephine Henning, who had rarely had the opportunity to partner each other in the season so far. Still, two such experienced defenders evidently needed little dress rehearsal to shine.

After four minutes of added time at the end of the second half, referee Sarah Garratt blew her whistle. Chelsea players dropped to the floor as the FA Cup winners cavorted around them. Stoney gave TV interviews with one of her toddler twins in each arm, then the players held hands and ran in a chain towards the fans behind the goal. Scott and Smith led the team up to the Royal Box, the former beaming, the latter looking delirious, and lifted the trophy together – presented to them by 14-year-old Maya Le Tissier, part of the England under-15 set-up as an incentive to encourage more girls and young women to take up the game.

Scott commented later that lifting the FA Cup at Wembley was a dream come true. Some 32,912 people watched the match inside the stadium, fewer than Emma Hayes had hoped for but more than had attended in 2015; millions more watched on television and listened on the radio. The Chelsea squad applauded their opponents, but none could manage to even dredge up a smile; the disappointment was written all over their faces. They were all professional enough to say afterwards that although they were upset, they knew the better team had won.

On the way out of Wembley, one of the security guards said that he had watched some of the match, and had enjoyed the goal. 'As good as any man!' he enthused.

Stage

AT a time when the ban on women's football had been all but forgotten by many, one theatre company decided in 2016 to remind people just how limited opportunities had been over the past century and beyond.

Off The Fence Theatre Company, with its artistic director Gary Phillpott, had been running workshops to create new writing on the topic of female opportunity. Phillpott had heard a sports historian talking on the radio about the 1921 ban and thought he must have misheard.

'I half-heard it, and had to go back to what he was saying,' Phillpott remembered. 'I disbelieved him – that in 1921 thousands and thousands of spectators watched two work teams play at Goodison Park. I thought this was talking about men, and it turned out that it was two female work teams playing, one of them being Dick, Kerr Ladies, and they attracted 50-odd thousand spectators. That was at a time when the average size of a First Division game, the Premiership now, was 10,000.

'As a sporty person, who's played football, cricket and rugby, why did I not know about women playing football? I thought it was the sort of thing that had started in the 70s and the 80s, through universities. Why didn't I know about it? Why was it so quiet? That became the springboard and we ended up putting the play together.'

Girls With Balls, as it became, had two incarnations – one play performed in 2015, and the other the year after, written by two different playwrights.

They shared a title and a rootedness in the history of Dick, Kerr Ladies, but nothing else. The 2016 version featured just four actors – three women and one man, each taking on dual roles, and all of the women playing footballers in the modern day and back in 1921. Perhaps it was unsurprising, but none of the trio had a football background in real life.

'They're all fit, sporty people,' pointed out Phillpott. 'They look as if they're footballers, they sound as if they're footballers, but if you put a ball at their feet and ask them to put it in the top left-hand corner, you would find woeful inadequacies – but they can act it. They are very fit, very active women – they certainly look and are very plausible, very believable as footballers.'

The play's first London performance was at the Broadway Theatre, Barking, in April 2016. It was an odd mixture of social realism (with footballers Ashley, Britney and Heather defending their soon-to-be-demolished clubhouse), period drama (flashing back to 1921 and the office of Alfred Frankland, general manager of Dick, Kerr Ladies, with players Lily Parr, Florrie Redford and Alice Kell looking on) and revenge tragedy (back in the present day, as the women's protest against demolition developed into something resembling Michael Winner's 1980s schlock-horror flick *Dirty Weekend* except with football boots on). With a small audience to start with, some began to filter out throughout the performance – perhaps they were expecting something a little more focused on women's football and its history.

Yet it had moments that rang exceptionally true. The trio of players were tormented by sexism in both eras – the modern women putting up with lascivious taunts while the trailblazers, famously, ended up being banned from playing altogether due to the edict that the game was physically 'unsuitable' for them.

Phillpott had already highlighted that the incidents of overt sexism triggered strong reactions from audiences, and often uncomfortable ones.

'Some of the laughter is interesting. There are some funny lines, and deliberately some funny lines; it's not a comedy and it's not playing for that, but there are one or two scenes where the man is quite sexist and there's laughter going around.

'When we first started getting laughs, we were thinking, "Why? Why are the audience laughing?" Is it embarrassment? Are some of the men identifying with that comment? Are some of the women laughing because they've heard it elsewhere and they know it goes on, and it's a way of recognition? Is it embarrassment, or is it that they genuinely think it's funny?'

On the play's first night in Barking, those laughs sounded like weary chuckles, the depressed acknowledgement that the women in the room had heard it all before. There did not seem to be much male laughter, though; perhaps the men had, like Phillpott, assumed that kind of behaviour had died out twenty or thirty years ago.

'One of our actors was saying she was running through the streets at six o'clock that morning and had been shouted at by three guys riding in a white van,' recounted Phillpott. 'Naively I thought that had stopped in about 1980, but I found out that it didn't.'

It was a neat touch that the play – not including its brief interval – lasted 90 minutes, but a shame, perhaps, that neither story got an actual conclusion. There is a fascinating story to be told about the Dick, Kerr Ladies that could be displayed beautifully on stage – of course, the limited amount of historical evidence might dissuade some playwrights, but the sheer drama of these women's lives and battles should be enough to inspire creativity.

As it is, *Girls with Balls* did make an important point – perhaps one it did not know it was making. The players – the Dick, Kerr pioneers and the modern girls – were just women: amateur, semi-professional, working-class, middle-class, manual workers, office workers, managers, mothers, wives, daughters, and friends – all brought together through the love of the game itself. These ordinary women did extraordinary things – the fictional women of 2016 forced into a situation where they took extreme action against their oppression, the real women of 1921 playing football (and essentially getting paid for it) even when the authorities tried to stop them.

In a blog published before the UK tour of the play began, actress Daisy Morris, who was taking on the roles of Lily Parr and Ashley, wrote, 'It would be nice to know the audience will learn a chunk of history that most people (myself included before the audition), have no idea about. I think it's an important part of history. It makes me wonder how incredible the skill would now be, in women footballers, in fact any sport that women have been told they shouldn't play or can't play, had they not been banned or deterred.'

Establishing the history of women's football is one step towards establishing its future.

To the future

AS the WPL prepared for the championship play-off, the WSL prepared for its break at the end of May and most other teams prepared for their summer holidays, the future structure of women's football was, as always, under discussion.

'I think they're going to go back to a winter league, which they need to do,' said one WSL2 administrator. 'Almost all the clubs want it.'

She admitted that there were clubs who thought that losing a summer league would also lose a sizeable proportion of the audience, and that a winter league during the men's season would create problems with access to the shared grounds.

Even that, though, would not be insurmountable. 'Our mid-season break will be like the Spanish – we'll have nothing over Christmas,' she suggested. 'I think that because we are so attuned to think that football is a winter sport, when it comes to summer and we're playing...'

She allowed herself a moment of irony as she considered outsiders' reactions to the way women's football was organised. 'People are like – what the hell?'

The FA were well aware of the challenges the women's game faced in the months and years to come. Kelly Simmons had already identified scheduling as a major problem –

particularly when the plan was to get more WSL matches televised.

'You're not going to get them on telly on a Sunday afternoon because you're going up against the busiest day in men's football,' she said. 'In an ideal world you'll end up with a TV slot which is probably going to end up being a night game, in reality, and all the other games played on your more traditional Sunday afternoon.

'We are in discussion with the clubs about when the season should run, there's a lot of challenges with running across the summer, and we do want to ultimately link the pyramid up for promotion and relegation. I think there's a lot to do as well around how the WSL runs and the fixtures to make it work for England, Champions League, the clubs and broadcasters and fans, obviously. The more we can get a regular slot for fans that's locked in and there's a run of fixtures the better.'

Some fans had expressed a concern about how competitive the 2016 WSL was likely to be, with a 'Big Three' of Chelsea, Arsenal and Manchester City identified from the off. Thumping scorelines such as City's 6-0 demolition of Doncaster Belles and Chelsea's 6-3 thrashing of Liverpool were reminiscent of the bad old days of women's football, when the talent was clustered at one or two clubs and the one-sidedness of matches reflected that. By the end of May, Manchester City were still unbeaten in the league and hadn't conceded a goal; Arsenal had already lost twice and had effectively ruled themselves out of the title; and though Chelsea were still clinging on by their fingertips, it looked like they would struggle to keep up with City.

However, Simmons pointed to the number of different WSL champions since its inception as an indicator that competition was still at a premium.

'It's gone to the last day of the season two years in a row – two years ago three teams could have won it on the last day,' she said. 'That's exactly what you want for the fans – you don't want someone to walk away with it year in year out.'

When the WSL had launched, there were strict financial controls on how much of a club's money could be spent on salaries, and how much any one player could earn. Those were relaxed, and it was a reasonable question whether or not these might be reintroduced, to stop a schism developing between the Big Three and the rest. Simmons was extremely wary about the prospect, reluctant to put a limit on players' earnings.

'We've got a soft cap in place to protect clubs' sustainability around turnover, but if you go to a hard cap, which is this thing that would ultimately drive a different split of players across the teams, that's a massive decision to make for those players – it's not a free market, you're not allowing players to earn the most they could earn.'

There were broader challenges to be dealt with all the way down the pyramid. The Girls' Football Weeks had proved a resounding success, taking everyone by surprise.

'We went for a 20 per cent increase but we've had over 50,000 girls take part in the week, which is fantastic,' said Simmons. 'When we launch our new strategy later this year, we want to double female participation. We need to encourage and support and incentivise clubs and schools to offer girls' football. We are really pleased with it. Obviously now we'll keep working hard with the partners that have come forward and got involved and see how we can support them going forward, but yes, great numbers.'

The WSL Sister Clubs project had been launched almost simultaneously, and Simmons was pleased too with the response to that.

'It's great,' she said. 'We want it to work both ways, really; we want the girls' teams to get behind and support the women's teams and be inspired as young players by them to keep playing and follow their dreams, but also to support their local clubs as well. It's a two-way partnership.'

The elite talent pathway had been restructured slightly with the establishment of regional talent centres – three tiers, spread across the country and attached to women's clubs. The licences for the centres had been awarded at the start of May 2016 as the FA explored ways to improve the development of young players, who would perhaps one day be the Lionesses of the future World Cups.

That was all well and good, but as the contrasting experiences of Goaldiggers and AFC Unity illustrated, investment in grassroots was also required; and the FA announced their intent to do that too, with plans to partner with other organisations – gym companies, for example – to provide accessible facilities, for men and women.

The FA also acknowledged the need to train more match officials as well as coaches – both critical to improve the standards in the women's game at all levels. Former England international Sue Lopez had written in 1996 that she and her colleagues had been encouraged in the mid-1970s to take coaching qualifications, and that the progress of women's football was hampered by the limited numbers of female coaches in the game – and in the intervening 20 years little progress had really been made.

During the summer of 2016, most sports turned their eyes towards Brazil and the imminent Olympic Games. In Great Britain's squad, however, there was a huge gap where the most popular participation sport in the country should have been. Although there had been a men's and women's squad representing Team GB at the London Olympics, that was a one-off. The football associations of the home nations could not reach an agreement that would allow the players to compete, for fear that their countries would not be able to compete individually at any other tournaments.

'I think it's a massive missed opportunity,' said Kelly Simmons. 'The English FA has been really clear, we wanted [Team GB for women's football] to happen. We were less bothered strategically about supporting the men's side because it's a youth competition, et cetera. It's not like the Olympics for women, which is a massive shop window for your sport in terms of profile, coverage and awareness, all those massive benefits that we've had before from the Olympics and the World Cup. It's a huge missed opportunity. The Scottish and the Welsh FA wouldn't entertain it.'

Simmons made it crystal-clear – just because the men were not going to compete, that should not rule out entering a women's squad.

'I think it's really important when we're looking at women's sport and women's football that we try not to always line it up against men, and say, "We don't do this for men, so we're not doing it for women,"' she said. 'We are playing catch-up from being banned, having no resources, no grounds, no support – we're playing massive catch-up. This nearly two million gap between girls and boys doing the required physical activity levels – it should be a national disgrace. So I just think that you just need to look at women's football through a different lens – women's *sport* through a different lens. Be more innovative, not always just say, "Well, in men's sport we do this." Find ways to make things happen, because you don't get many of those opportunities. Personally, I just think for those players, who work so unbelievably hard, haven't had some of the advantages that male footballers have, they've had to work phenomenally hard, balance their careers and training to get to the very top – to deny them…I don't agree with it.'

The players likely to be involved in any Olympic squad were diplomatic about the ongoing battles.

'It's a hard one for us as players,' said England vice-captain Jordan Nobbs. 'It's very disappointing. We want to be allowed to compete in the Olympics because of how far we got in the World Cup and we'd love that to happen, we'd love to be competing in major tournaments, that's the only way we can keep highlighting the women's game, let us play in major tournaments like that. Us as players, there's not a lot else we can do apart from playing well on the football pitch.'

Simmons did, however, suggest that they needed to make their opinions a little clearer.

'When we come back to talking about it again, which we inevitably will, it's important that everyone who thinks it should happen is really vocal about it, because I think we've got to have a full debate with all the stakeholders in the game,' she said. 'The players are the biggest stakeholders. We're all here for the players, that's why we exist, to provide football for those players at whatever level that is. I'd like to see a really open debate about what's best for women's football – and women's sport.'

The players, from elite to grassroots, were clear that although much had been achieved in recent years, there was much still to do. Some, like Arsenal's Alex Scott, felt they had a responsibility themselves to progress the game as far as they could. Even her media appearances, she said, were chosen carefully not just to raise her own profile but to raise the profile of her club and her sport.

'The main thing that has changed is attitudes to women's football now,' she said. 'Even when you go into your local supermarket now, attitudes have changed. You get grown men coming up and saying, "I'm so proud of you girls, you've done well," whereas before you never used to get that. It used to be your stereotypical comments about "get back in the kitchen", that sort of thing, but now you have people genuinely coming up to you and are proud of what you've actually achieved.

'When I started, when I was eight, I had baggy kit and was only training twice a week – to see how far women's football has come…' She paused, and added, 'And we're not *there* yet. That's the thing. We can't get comfortable and sit on what we've done. It's about still trying to move this sport forward in all areas.'

Epilogue

SOMETIMES sport is still depressingly stuck in the dark
ages when it comes to gender equality.

In the same week in May that golf club Muirfield
voted to continue excluding female members, West Ham
United went back on their agreement to allow the women's
team to play one last game at the Boleyn Ground. The men
had played their final match there against Manchester
United, inviting alumni along to bid farewell to the old place,
but the ground was still going to be there for some months,
with amateur sides and corporate hires scheduled over the
summer.

For the fans, however, the women's team playing there
under the West Ham banner was a step too far. They only
wanted to raise some money to keep going but public outrage
was apparently so high that permission for the women to
say goodbye to the historic ground was withdrawn. It was
incredibly disappointing all round.

Yet as I wrote this book and continued to report for
newspapers and websites, I noticed some changes in attitude
around the country.

A lot more people were interested in women's football
than I had ever known before. When I mentioned the likes
of Steph Houghton or Lucy Bronze, my friends or colleagues
knew who I meant. Those who hadn't watched the game

before tuned in to England matches; I got texts and Twitter messages asking me about players and their careers. That was both cheering and a little disheartening – nobody needs to ask me about the men's England captain Wayne Rooney, because they've known all about him since he was a teenager, from his playing style to his injury record; but Steph Houghton, even with her picture on the front pages in the summers of 2012 and 2015, was still an unknown quantity. I was providing some necessary context that the uninitiated would have no idea how to access.

Yet women's football in England remains a rather guarded, inward-looking sphere. One has to know where to look to find out about players or fixtures, and has to put in a great deal of effort to get to even a top-flight fixture. When England played Belgium at Rotherham's New York Stadium in April, my sister watched it on the BBC, and heard the pundits talk about the next fixture – away to Bosnia, four days later. She messaged me to ask if that match was on the TV too.

I replied, 'No.'

'Why show one and not the other? Ridiculous!'

My response? 'Welcome to my world.'

Even though the reasons might be excellent, fundamentally the media coverage of women's football is still limited – and that's a strategic decision in some cases, like the England broadcasts.

I saw lots of comments during the season from fans asking why journalists weren't covering more women's football. In my experience, it can be simply because editors aren't commissioning the pieces; a staff journalist might get sent to a men's game instead, or a freelancer decides to cover something that's definitely going to get published and thus get them paid.

Sometimes, however, and it's a touch sad to say, journalists are trying their very best to report on what's happening, and to secure interviews and access behind the scenes, but clubs and the governing bodies reject the requests. Whether that's because they want to keep the players and staff protected from the media glare, or it's simply because they don't have the people on hand to deal with journalists' enquiries appropriately, I'm still not sure.

Sometimes the problems are simply down to the women's game remaining subservient to the men's. As mentioned earlier, Arsenal Ladies rearranged their crunch WSL fixture against title-holders Chelsea on a Thursday evening in April, shifting kick-off time from the usual 7.45pm to a maddening 6pm.

Having the match so early in the evening meant many fans were not able to travel to Boreham Wood in time – and all because the club wanted to give people the chance to watch the men play West Brom later on, but on the television rather than in person. Talking to staff at various clubs, in many places the terminology is still 'the first team' to refer to the men, and 'the ladies' to refer to the women – just as the FA runs 'the FA Cup' and 'the Women's FA Cup', and FIFA host 'the World Cup' and 'the Women's World Cup'. The men's game is the norm; the women's game needs to have a qualifying term tagged on.

Indeed, there is potentially also a problem with the pipeline of talent – not as players, but as coaches and match officials. Emma Hayes might have led her Chelsea side to the double in 2015, but all the other managers of WSL1 teams that season were men.

The referees and assistants even at WSL games are usually men as well – and just as WSL grounds and facilities are equivalent to men's non-league level, the match officials and their officiating experience are too.

Thus there is the rather odd imbalance where England's top professional female players are having their livelihoods affected directly by enthusiastic amateurs. This was the case in the men's game too not so long ago – anyone who watched football a couple of decades ago will remember referees being introduced along with their usual occupations (I remember George Courtney and David Elleray being school teachers) – but it is indicative of the huge challenges still facing women's football in England.

Yet a new generation of fans are growing up watching women's football alongside the men's game. Sometimes because it's there on the television, sometimes because it's close to their homes and the ticket prices are affordable, and sometimes because the clubs themselves are working so incredibly hard to attract people to the ground, with players visiting schools and local community groups as well as prize-givings at junior clubs – and the Sister Clubs project is the natural progression of that.

In 2016, I took my five-year-old nephew to his first football match. He already knew that I wrote about women's football, and going to a game seemed the obvious next step. He was instantly hooked – not because of what happened on the pitch, necessarily, but because of everything around it, from the kids' activities to the mascots to the half-time competition (which he won, picking up a shirt as his prize, and promptly asking his parents for the rest of the strip too). Two weeks later he went to his second football match – wearing his new kit.

It can be as simple as that, getting a child's buy-in – but they'll need an adult to accompany them, and adults sometimes need a little more persuasion. They won't be lured to a ground with the promise of kicking a ball around at the front of the terrace, like my nephew was; they might not fancy standing on cold concrete behind a goal; and the ever-changing kick-off times making it difficult to keep track of what's happening could well put them off permanently. The quality of play in the elite women's game might be attractive; the quality of grounds and officiating, both at the equivalent of the men's non-league level, might be off-putting. They might ask the question – if this isn't being taken seriously and treated as elite professional sport by the governing bodies and the clubs, then why should the rest of us take it seriously and treat it as elite professional sport?

Yet things are changing – and progressing, slowly but surely. Many established football fans – no matter how committed – are unaware of the ban that stopped the growth of the women's game a century ago.

When I'm asked why women's football is still on the up and seen as a niche sport, I talk about the ban and the later lack of interest and investment from the authorities, and, in general, people are shocked. Why have they not heard about this before, they wonder?

And it's the same question they ask about the game now. Why don't they know about the fixtures in the Women's Super League? Why don't they know about the garlanded playing careers of the likes of current England assistant coach Marieanne Spacey, or Hall of Famer Gillian Coultard, or Manchester City Women's ambassador Sylvia Gore, or the legendary Lily Parr, with a strike so hard she is said to have broken a man's arm with the impact? The coverage and chronicling of women's football has been historically lacklustre and limited.

I like to think that things are changing now. It may be slow and steady progress – but this is perhaps for the best. Women's football in England has always had firm roots. Now it is gradually branching out as well, growing into something to be proud of – top to bottom.

A small group of committed enthusiasts kept the women's game alive for most of the 20th century. In the 21st century, that group is growing, and becoming more professional – forcing their way into long-closely-guarded spaces, getting the sport noticed, and making more and more noise. The England team may grab headlines, the players in the Women's Super League may be the full-time professionals, but they benefit from the investment and passion of their fans and the endeavours of those throughout the pyramid – and those who came before them, who sustained the game for so many years with so little help and so little attention.

We are all Lionesses. Hear us roar.

ABOUT THE AUTHOR

MICHAEL KOGGE'S original work includes *Empire of the Wolf*, an epic graphic novel about werewolves in ancient Rome. He also is the author of the junior novel for *The Force Awakens* and *Batman v Superman: Cross Fire*, a companion novel.

He can be found online at www.MichaelKogge.com.